JUDY TURNER AND MARGARET ROLFE

SUCCESSFUL SCRAP QUILTS

FROM SIMPLE RECTANGLES

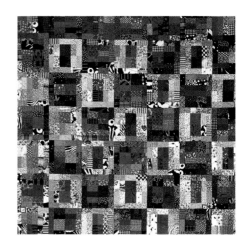

ACKNOWLEDGMENTS

In 1997 I began teaching a patchwork workshop based on Japanese tatami mat arrangements. When I witnessed the enthusiasm and wonderful quilts produced by my students, I realized the potential of this simple idea. However, this potential would not have evolved into a book without the collaboration of Margaret Rolfe and her thoughtful insight and encouragement. For this, I sincerely thank her.

I would particularly like to thank Libby Hepburn, Tracey Smith, Jenny Bowker, Karen Merchant, Di Mansfield, and my sister, Barbara Gower, for allowing their wonderful quilts to be photographed. Christopher Keen and Rollo and Joc Brett kindly lent quilts from their collections also.

I am grateful to Barbara Gower and to Susan Campbell from Rowdy Flat Quilting for their excellent machine quilting.

The support of my family, especially the wonderful cooking of my husband, Ian, allowed me the time and space to give this book my full attention. The sometimes succinct color advice from my son, Nicholas, was also appreciated.

—Judy Turner

I was immediately enthusiastic when Judy invited me to work with her on this book. I welcomed the opportunity to collaborate with a friend whose work I admired, and I was grateful for the chance to further explore the enchantment of scrap quilts. It has been a happy and fruitful collaboration, and I thank Judy for this.

My thanks to Beth Reid, who so expertly machine quilted many quilts for me, and also to Jackie MacNab, of Brindabella Quilting, for her lovely quilting of my "Bondi Beach" quilt.

I am grateful to my husband, Barry, for his continual support of my quiltmaking and book writing.

—Margaret Rolfe

CREDITS

President · *Nancy J. Martin*
CEO · *Daniel J. Martin*
Publisher · *Jane Hamada*
Editorial Director · *Mary V. Green*
Managing Editor · *Tina Cook*
Technical Editor · *Darra Williamson*
Copy Editor · *Liz McGehee*
Design Director · *Stan Green*
Illustrator · *Robin Strobel*
Cover and Text Designer · *Trina Stahl*
Quilt Photographer · *Andrew Sikorski*
Studio Photographer · *Brent Kane*

Successful Scrap Quilts from Simple Rectangles
© 2002 by Judy Turner and Margaret Rolfe

That Patchwork Place® is an imprint of Martingale & Company™.

Martingale & Company
20205 144th Ave. NE
Woodinville, WA 98072-8478
www.martingale-pub.com

Printed in Singapore
07 06 05   8 7 6 5

Library of Congress Cataloging-in-Publication Data
Turner, Judy.
    Successful scrap quilts from simple rectangles / Judy Turner and Margaret Rolfe.
        p. cm.
    ISBN 1-56477-386-8
    1. Patchwork—Patterns. 2. Quilting—Patterns. 3. Rectangle in art. I. Rolfe, Margaret. II. Title.

TT835 .R6535 2002
746.46'041—dc21   2001057913

MISSION STATEMENT
We are dedicated to providing quality products and service by working together to inspire creativity and to enrich the lives we touch.

CONTENTS

INTRODUCTION

Glory be to God for dappled things—
For skies of couple-colour as a brinded cow;
For rose-moles all in stipple upon trout that swim;
Fresh-firecoal chestnut-falls; finches' wings;
Landscape plotted and pieced—fold, fallow,
    and plough;
And all trades, their gear and tackle and trim.

From "Pied Beauty" by Gerard Manley Hopkins (1844–89)

S CRAP QUILTS are among the most beloved of all styles of quilt-making. There is an enduring appeal in quilts that make our eyes rove over their surface, delighting in the constant changes of print and color, even as an underlying pattern helps lend order and make sense of the variety. The pattern repeats—yet is different—in each repetition because of the many fabrics used.

Scrap quilts are a joy to make, from the process of collecting all the pieces of fabric to the satisfaction in choosing the constantly changing juxtapositions of fabrics within the design. Often, fabrics in scrap quilts are pieces left over from other quiltmaking or dressmaking projects, so the patches evoke all kinds of memories. Fabrics can be treasures, collected on our travels or given to us by friends; they can remind us of special people or events. We often collect particular colors or kinds of prints, and our stashes overflow with small pieces that we have hoarded over many years. Scrap quilts are a wonderful way to use these accumulations of precious pieces. Scrap quilts are timeless and charming, and add a special touch to any decor. Scrap quilts warm people's hearts as well as their bodies.

We have been longtime friends through quilt-making, and we both have always loved scrap quilts. From the beginning of her quiltmaking career, Judy sought to include the widest possible variety of fabric in her quilts. The seemingly endless potential of print fabrics to shade through color and depth of tonal value led her to explore quilts that focused on shading with strips. Colorwash quilts were a logical extension to this work, leading to her book *Awash with Colour* (That Patchwork Place, 1997).

Margaret came to scrap quilts from a different angle, as her first love involved the exploration of pattern. However, she quickly realized that repetitive patterns became much more exciting when she used a variety of fabrics. The animal quilts in her previously published books, *Go Wild with Quilts* and *A Quilter's Ark* (That Patchwork Place, 1993 and 1997), benefited from the wide use of fabrics from her ever-expanding stash. In addition, Margaret collaborated with Judy Hooworth to write *Spectacular Scraps* (That Patchwork Place, 1999), which presents a fresh approach to scrap quilts based on applying two color families to simple triangle-based designs, a concept that Judy Hooworth developed.

Successful Scrap Quilts offers some totally new designs for making scrap quilts. The inspiration comes from arrangements of thick straw mats, called tatami, which are traditionally used as floor coverings in Japanese homes. Rooms are literally designed around arrangements of these mats, with the room size determined by the number of tatami.

Judy discovered various arrangements of tatami mats in a book on Japanese design, *The Japanese Home Stylebook* (Stonebridge Press, 1992), illustrated by Saburo Yamagata. The diagrams caught her quiltmaker's eye because of the mat's rectangular shape—essentially a short strip. Judy saw that these mat arrangements could be adapted for patchwork, with the simple rectangle as the basis for a whole variety of brand-new one-patch quilt patterns. Within the basic arrangement of rectangles, pieces could be shaded to create a specific block design. By repeating, reversing, and rotating the shaded blocks or making them in opposite combinations of dark and light values, the design possibilities become endless. A single arrangement of rectangles might yield many block designs, depending upon how the rectangles are shaded. The rectangle has the added bonus of being very simple to cut and sew, with no bias edges or difficult measurements.

Beyond the possibilities of the new block designs lies a deeper issue. What actually makes scrap quilts work? Many books offer scrap-quilt projects, but very few of them actually explain the mechanics of what makes a scrap quilt successful. In this book, we explore the fundamentals of how pattern is created through contrast and how the dimensions of tonal value, color, and print contribute to the success of the quilt. Understanding these factors will help you choose the best patchwork design to showcase your particular collection of fabrics.

The scrap quilts in this book are perfect for today's quiltmaker, as they use current tools and methods of quiltmaking. Rectangles are cut accurately and efficiently with that miracle of modern quiltmaking, the rotary cutter, and are sewn together quickly by machine. The quilts, which consist of hundreds of small pieces, also lend themselves to quilting by machine, either via free-motion stitching or with simple lines.

> "... many quilts that capture both our eyes and heart were created from the scrap bag."
>
> From *Threads of Time*
> by Nancy J. Martin
> (That Patchwork Place, 1990),
> page 52.

SUCCESSFUL SCRAP QUILTS

BEFORE YOU begin to stitch scrap quilts from the specific block designs in this book, it helps to review the basic characteristics of successful scrap quilts in general. A greater understanding of the theory behind these multifabric quilts will help you approach making the quilts in this book, as well as all kinds of scrap quilts.

LEARNING FROM THE PAST

SCRAP QUILTS made in the past are greatly valued, and we love to collect them. In general, the women who made them did more sewing than we do today, but it is important to recall that they usually worked from a narrower range of fabrics than what is now available. The fabrics our foremothers used were scraps left over from their dressmaking and home sewing, so they tended to reflect the fashion of that specific time—fashion which changed a bit more slowly in those days. These "fashionable" fabrics give vintage quilts their special look, so that today we can recognize them as being from the '30s, the turn of the century, or whenever.

For example, when grandma made her quilts during the 1930s and 1940s, she worked from a scrap bag full of bits and pieces from her dresses and aprons, from the children's clothes she made, and perhaps from feed sacks that she bought. Her fabrics would have been largely in colors popular at the time, such as the familiar Nile green, lilac, peach, and pastel blues. The print styles would also be typical of the era, with lots of white backgrounds and white "halos" surrounding the motifs.

The same applies to great-grandma's quilts, made at the turn of the twentieth century when women used fabrics in colors such

Detail of scrap quilt, maker unknown, United States, circa 1930–40. Collection of Judy Turner.

as black, indigo blue, maroon, and purple. Prints were typically small repeating patterns. Great-great-grandma, working in the 1870s, had yet a different palette of color and prints: cinnamon browns, bubble-gum pinks, and strange shades of yellow-green. And so it goes back in time through the generations.

There is another side to this story of old quilts. Often in the past, quiltmakers lacked ready access to quantities of new fabric. Perhaps they could not get to a store easily, or if they could, they may not have been able to buy much fabric. They couldn't go to a quilt store for "just the right green" as we are able to do. They generally used what they had in their scrap bag, making do with what they found there. If they ran out of a green print, they would simply substitute another. They made unexpected choices and combined different prints and colors. Often, when we look closely at these older quilts, we are surprised by some of the odd fabrics and combinations. Yet the quilts "work"; in fact, they

have vitality because they are not perfectly matched. The substitutions and juxtapositions in these old quilts increase their visual interest.

There seems to be a contradiction here, and it is a contradiction that goes to the very heart of making successful scrap quilts. On the one hand, it is good to have unity in the overall look of a quilt, and old quilts have this unity, being largely made from fabrics fashionable at the time. On the other hand, a quilt is more interesting and vital if everything is not too perfectly matched, as in the past when quiltmakers used whatever fabric they happened to have.

Today, most of us do less sewing for ourselves, for our homes, and for our families. But we do make quilts and collect fabrics for our quilts. There is a whole industry devoted to creating special fabrics for quiltmaking, generating new designs as well as copying old ones. To supplement this, we also can use current dressmaking fabrics—just as our grandmothers did—as well as fabrics intended for home furnishings, and ethnic fabrics from the increasingly international nature of our world. The result is a huge range of fabrics, either already in our stash or available for us to buy.

This bounty can be both a blessing and a problem. It is a blessing in that we can enjoy making choices from the abundance of wonderful fabrics. We mostly needn't pine for the "just right" print missing from our stash. On the other hand, it is easy to become overwhelmed with choices and not know where to begin. We often don't know where to end either, lacking the confidence to say "no" to a fabric. We sometimes think that we should use anything and everything in our scrap quilts, but in fact this is not so. Successful scrap quilts generally have some thread that lends unity to the whole. This quick and easy access to the "perfect" fabric can also lead us to overmatch and overcoordinate, eliminating prints or colors that might add that extra spark to our quilt.

In this book, we offer you guidance in two

areas. First, we offer the tools to give your scrap quilt the unity and coherence that it needs so it does not descend into chaos, or have the odd patch that stands out like a soldier out of step. And second, we suggest methods to make and integrate variations so the eye is always interested and eager to travel over the quilt without boredom.

Understanding the Fundamentals

THERE IS an accepted wisdom that scrap quilts are made by creating a design from a specific arrangement of dark and light fabrics. The reality, however, is not quite that simple. In fact, *scrap quilts work by creating a pattern through some kind of contrast.* Usually it is a contrast in value, but it also may be a contrast in color or style of print.

Let's explore these three key elements that underlie successful scrap quilts: the dimensions of tonal value, color, and style of printed fabrics. Understanding these three elements and how they work together will help you create richer and more interesting scrap quilts.

Tonal Value

THE CONCEPT of tonal value is very important in scrap quilts. Tonal value (often simply called value)

Two tonal-value scales: white-to-black scale and scale with colors

refers to the degree of darkness or lightness in the color of the fabric. Obviously, white and black are the extremes of tonal value, with white being the lightest and black being the darkest. All other colors fit somewhere between these two extremes. Arranging things according to lightness and darkness creates what is called a "tonal scale." Prints—which can combine one, two, or many colors—also can be arranged into a tonal scale.

It is important to note that tonal value can be relative. The same fabric might appear light in one situation, where it has dark neighbors, but dark in a situation where its neighbors are light.

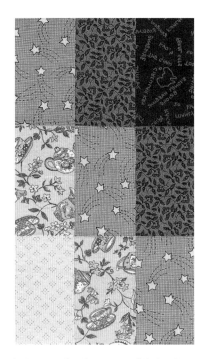

Relative tonal value: same fabric (the star fabric) as light, medium, and dark

Determining Tonal Value

Any group of fabrics can be arranged in a scale of tonal value by lining them up from light to dark, with 1" (2.5 cm) or so of each fabric visible. Stand back from the arrangement and squint your eyes. Do any fabrics stand out? Shuffle them around until the arrangement looks right. Are there any interruptions in the range; that is, do certain fabrics stand out from the others by creating a vertical "stripe" when you run your eyes over the arrangement? Looking through either a reducing glass or a camera lens can help you clarify the order. If you wear glasses, take them off and study the range. Sometimes it helps to walk away from the group of fabrics, then come back later to look at it with fresh eyes.

Fabrics arranged by tonal value:
one with "stripe" and one without

Value and Scrap Quilts

In scrap quilts, the pattern is usually—although not always—carried by the dark and light values. The repetition of the dark and light values in the same place in each block usually provides the contrast that creates the overall pattern. If the dark and light contrast is not maintained, the pattern becomes lost, and the design descends into chaos.

Beyond the value contrast that creates the basic pattern, it is important to look at the values *within* the light and dark areas of the pattern. If all the darks are exactly the same degree of value, and all the lights are exactly the same degree of value as well, the quilt becomes monotonous. Look at the block at the upper right and see how flat it looks.

Block with exactly the same degree of
values in light and dark areas

So, while the pattern in a scrap quilt may well be established by the lights and darks, it is how the values are varied *within* the areas of light and dark that makes scrap quilts more successful and interesting. The introduction of a range of relative values within the dark and light areas can create all kinds of fascinating variations on the basic pattern. Your quilt will be richer if your choices within the dark and light fabrics come from a range of tonal values. Now view the same block, this time with a range of values appearing within the light and dark areas.

Identical block with a range of dark
and light fabrics included

Remember that value is relative, and that the same fabric can act as both a dark and a light, depending on its neighbors in the design. These "chameleon" fabrics are usually medium in value, so medium-value prints have an important place in scrap quilts. If you study the detail of "Spectrum" shown below, you'll notice a dark blue block with a red center in the middle of the bottom row. In this block, the red acts as a light in the center of the dark block. In the row above, the red acts as a dark in the center of a light block.

Detail of "Spectrum." For full view of quilt, see page 69.

The patterns in scrap quilts do not have to be made from just two contrasting areas of value. Patterns can be created with three, or sometimes even more, areas of value. For example, in "Autumn Stars" (page 62), Judy used two values of beige prints for different areas of light in the quilt. In "French Connections" (page 34), Libby Hepburn used three different tonal values.

COLOR

WHEN WE look at quilts, we usually react first to the color. Color and tonal value always interact together, but it is important that we separate them here so that we better understand how they work.

If only one color is used, all the variations of light and dark are within that single color; this is called a monochromatic color scheme. For example, if blue is the chosen color, then the dark areas should be various values of dark blue, and the light areas should be various values of light blue, as well as blue-and-white mixtures that read as light blue. For examples of monochromatic schemes, see "Something Blue" (page 30) and "French Connections" (page 34).

Just two colors can also make great scrap quilts. There are wonderful possibilities for using two colors: blue and yellow, pink and green, and hot pink and black are just some of the combinations we used. By choosing two colors, you will usually be following the principle of tonal value creating the pattern, as generally one color is darker than the other, with blue being darker than yellow, green being darker than pink, and so on. However, you can also make marvelous scrap quilts with just a contrast of color carrying the pattern. The quilts in Margaret's previous book with Judy Hooworth, *Spectacular Scraps*, reflect this approach.

Multicolored quilts have the potential of great richness. Again, dark and light colors create the pattern, with the variety of colors creating interest. Since the colors themselves vary in value, a range of value is assured within the light and dark areas of the pattern. The different colored prints used for the dark areas of "An Old-Fashioned Quilt" (page 56) are an example.

You can increase visual interest in a scrap quilt by varying the color itself within the quilt. If you are using red, for instance, don't always use the same shade of red, but vary it by adding orange-reds and blue-reds, or even substituting some orange prints and purple prints for the reds. Don't match the colors completely. Introduce lighter and darker tints and shades, and colors that are related. In Judy's quilt "Flush of Spring" (page 59), the greens vary from blue-green through touches of yellow-green or olive green, as seen on page 11.

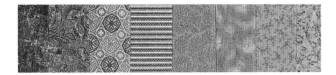

Range of green fabrics from "Flush of Spring"

Beige is a popular choice for creating light areas in quilts. However, many beige fabrics "read" the same, even though their prints are different. Consider introducing some other colors to your range of lights, such as soft pinks or blues. Notice in the detail below of Margaret's "An Old-Fashioned Quilt" how the pink prints scattered among the beiges add a touch of warmth to the quilt.

Similarly, black is often used as a dark color in a quilt. Consider instead adding dark navy blues and purples for depth. Judy did this in her quilt "Two Yellow Canaries" (page 49), as not all the prints have a black background. Margaret also included navy prints with the black prints in her quilt "Lava Flow" (page 87).

Touches of bright or clear colors will add a spark to your quilt. These are the accents that make a quilt lively and visually interesting. To use a cooking analogy, these are the spices that add that extra zing to the recipe. But as with spice, too much can ruin the stew! Be sparing with the accent colors, adding just enough, but not too much. For a good balance, see the reds used as accents in Margaret's "An Old-Fashioned Quilt" on page 56. In the detail below of Judy's "Two Yellow Canaries," the yellow adds the accent in a largely black-and-pink quilt.

Detail of "An Old-Fashioned Quilt,"
showing beige plus pink prints used as lights.
For full view of quilt, see page 56.

Detail of "Two Yellow Canaries," showing a yellow
accent. For full view of quilt, see page 49.

STYLE OF PRINTED FABRICS

BEYOND BOTH value and color, there is the dimension of the style of print on fabrics. (We call fabrics with the absence of print *solids*.) Nowadays, printed fabrics come in every possible style: large and small motifs, geometrics and florals, spots and stripes, checks and plaids, pictorial and abstract, contemporary and reproduction.

Prints and solids can be combined to create pattern in a scrap quilt. The prints can define one part of the design and the solids another. For example, in "Board Short Boogie-Woogie" (page 31), the bright solids form a contrast to the busy contemporary prints. In the detail of "Down Memory Lane" below, the cream solid fabric contrasts nicely with the busy '30s prints.

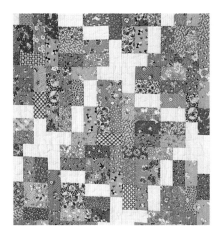

Detail of "Down Memory Lane," showing contrast between printed and solid fabrics. For full view of quilt, see page 66.

Completely opposite approaches can be used with regard to print fabrics in scrap quilts. On the one hand, prints can be varied to create interest. Checks and stripes can be included among florals and tone-on-tones as Judy did with the pink fabrics in "Flush of Spring" (page 59). Alternatively, prints can be kept the same or very similar, such as the tone-on-tones used in "Spectrum" (page 69) or the checks and plaids in "Checkerboard" (page 78). In these two quilts, the tonal values make the contrast that creates the pattern. Interest is created through the variety of colors rather than through the style of prints.

A quick and easy way to increase your fabric options is to use the reverse side of your print fabrics. Turn each print over and see if the other side reveals a lighter value, a softer pattern, or some variation that will be useful in the quilt. Judy often uses the reverse side of prints to add variation to her quilts. For instance, she used both sides of many of the Japanese prints in "Bento Box" (page 84), and both sides of most of the fabrics in "Spectrum" (page 69).

Examine the wrong sides of your fabrics for additional fabric options.

Bringing It All Together

We have analyzed the theory behind scrap quilts in terms of the contrast that creates pattern, and the roles of tonal value, color, and style of print. How you bring these aspects together is what makes your scrap quilt unique. The following hints will give you some additional principles to guide you.

Repetition and Variation

Essentially, all that we have said about scrap quilts can be summed up in two words: repetition and variation. The pattern in a scrap quilt is created by the *repetition* of a block that has a contrast within it, but the interest in the pattern is created by the *variation* you bring to those repetitions. Sometimes the pattern may become a little blurred by the variation, but even this can add interest.

> Remember, scrap quilts are a balancing act! While too little variation results in boredom, too much variation can result in confusion and chaos. The ideal is to have just the right amount of variation to keep the eye interested, but not so much that the overall design is lost or overwhelmed.

Variety Is Important

In general, "more is more" with scrap quilts. The greater the variety of fabrics you bring to your quilt, the richer it will be. Small amounts of a wide range of fabrics add depth and interest. In her quilt "Black and White and Red All Over" (page 52), Judy used a total of 228 prints! Not much of each print was used, but by using so many prints, Judy has created a quilt that is a pleasure to see and study. She even included some prints commemorating the new millennium, which will surely delight the fabric historian of the future.

Some fabrics, especially large prints, can look quite different when cut into smaller pieces. Just cutting from different areas of the print can yield totally different results. Cutting fabrics in different directions, such as cutting a stripe so that it runs horizontally or vertically, creates variation as well.

We stress, however, that we are not suggesting an "anything goes" approach. The fabrics should always fit within your chosen scheme. Trust your eyes to tell you when something goes a bit too far.

> Swapping small amounts of fabric with friends is a wonderful way to achieve more variety in your fabric collection. As an added bonus, you will always remember your friends through the pieces they gave you.

Fabric Placement: Scattering and Blending

We have established that pattern in scrap quilts is created by the repetition of areas of contrast. Now we must consider how to place the fabrics *within* these areas.

There are two different approaches to placing fabrics within the areas that create the pattern of a block design: scattering and blending. Study the two blocks on page 14. Both are made from exactly the same fabrics. Contrast in the blocks is created by the pinks, which form the light values, and the greens, which form the dark values. In Block A, the various values and shades of pink and green are scattered. In Block B, the various values and shades of pink and green are blended, so the color and value appear to "flow" around the block.

A   B

Two blocks illustrating scattered color (A)
and blended color (B)

Scattering

As the name implies, scattering mixes the tonal values, colors, or prints in a random fashion throughout the areas of contrast within the block. When scattering, avoid placing any two pieces of similar value, color, or print next to each other. The aim is to vary the mix as much as possible. For examples, see "Black and White and Red All Over," a detail of which is shown below, "An Old-Fashioned Quilt" (page 56), and "Checkerboard" (page 78).

Detail of "Black and White and Red All Over,"
showing scattered tonal values, colors, and prints.
For full view of quilt, see page 52.

Scattering also comes into play as you stitch the blocks to complete the quilt top. Always check that repeating or accent fabrics are sprinkled over the entire quilt rather than grouped in one area.

Blending

When blending, place fabrics with similar characteristics side by side, making a smooth transition from one to the next. This approach is the same as that used in colorwash quilts. It is an approach that can be used to make lovely variations within scrap quilts, and it works especially well for some of the designs in this book.

With this approach, each piece in the design needs to be placed carefully in relation to its neighbors. There are three ways that pieces can be blended. The first is by matching or nearly matching the color in adjacent pieces, or by keeping the color the same but changing the value to a slightly lighter or darker shade.

Blending with the same color

A second way to blend is to change the color but maintain the value. For instance, a blue and a red piece might be placed side by side, and if they are the same or very similar in value, they will have the effect of flowing smoothly from one to another.

Blending with colors of the same value

Finally, you may use the pattern on the print to make the blend for you. For example, you may place a floral with a green leaf next to a green print of the same or similar shade or value. In effect, the color "bleeds" from one patch into its neighbor.

Blending through "bleeding"

It is best to work on a design wall (see page 38) when you are attempting to blend fabrics. This allows you to consider each piece as it is placed in the design to ensure that the colors and/or values flow smoothly from one piece to the next.

For examples of effective blending, see "Spectrum" (page 69), "Flush of Spring" (page 59), and "Todd's Quilt" (page 34). The latter

moves the color across the quilt by clever blending between neighboring blocks.

PUTTING THEORY INTO PRACTICE

THEORY IS all very well, but in practice, how should you proceed? The following is a step-by-step approach.

GATHER THE FABRICS

A COMFORTABLE way to begin a scrap quilt is to establish a theme or a color scheme and then choose prints to fit your plan. Judy chose a seasonal theme and a pink-and-green color scheme for "Flush of Spring" (page 59). Color itself was the key to "Black and White and Red All Over" (page 52), which includes a wide selection of prints in black, white, and red. Two colors—blue and yellow—inspired "Bondi Beach" (page 75), while a particular type of print—checked and plaid geometrics—provided the starting point for "Checkerboard" (page 78).

In a similar fashion, you may enjoy using your collection of reproduction fabrics, as in "Down Memory Lane" (page 66), which uses '30s-style prints, or "An Old-Fashioned Quilt" (page 56), which features prints reminiscent of the Civil War era. Special occasions, such as Christmas, can provide a theme, as in "Christmas Lanterns" (page 93), while brightly colored and/or juvenile prints can be combined effectively, as demonstrated in "1-2-3 What Can You See?" (page 81).

Predetermining a theme, a color scheme, or a specific collection of fabrics does not mean that you cannot introduce other prints. For example, you can extend your collection of Christmas prints with other red and green prints in your stash. Non-reproduction fabrics can work well with reproduction prints if they fit the general "feeling" or color scheme.

Always begin by looking at your own fabric stash. Do you have lots of a particular color or style of print? Do you have a collection of special fabrics? It is surprising what you can pull from your own stash once you have chosen a starting point.

Then it's time to go shopping! Since you have established a theme or a color scheme and know what you already have on hand, you will have more confidence in selecting from today's wonderful variety of fabrics. You'll also have a specific direction upon which to focus your shopping. You do not need to buy large quantities of any one fabric for scrap quilts. Small pieces, such as fat quarters, are ideal.

ORGANIZE THE FABRICS TO CREATE CONTRAST

NEXT, ESTABLISH how you will create the contrast in your scrap quilt. The most common approach is through the arrangement of light and dark fabrics, but it could also be the contrast of prints against solids, or perhaps one color against another. In "Two Yellow Canaries" (page 49), Judy decided that pink print fabrics would create the ideal contrast to the black and multicolored fabrics. When making "Down Memory Lane" (page 66), Margaret chose a solid cream-colored fabric to contrast with her light-colored but busy '30s prints.

Sort the fabrics into two or three piles, categorizing them by the characteristic you will be using to create the contrast in your design, such as light and dark or different colors. Working one pile at a time, arrange the fabrics one behind the other so that about 1" (2.5 cm) of each fabric shows, creating a run that blends them together as a whole. Generally, this means arranging them by tonal values. (For a refresher, see "Determining Tonal Value" on page 8.)

Take a long look at what is happening in each run. Do the fabrics work together? Do any stand out, and if so, why? Alternatively, does the run lack "spice"; that is, are all the fabrics too similar in color, value, or print? Do they need an accent? Will more medium (or darker, or lighter) values add variety?

You don't have to like a fabric to use it in the quilt. You don't even have to like two particular fabrics together for them to work in the quilt. Odd fabrics and odd combinations can work very well when combined with your other fabrics, often providing that little bit of dissonance that creates visual interest and variation. So if you are using blue, all the blues don't have to match. If they do, you will create a quilt that looks just like a single purchased piece of fabric! Remember what we said about color, and introduce some different shades.

Judy has two nice little rules to help you along.

1. *Every fabric needs two friends.* If you have fabrics that stand out too much on their own, they can be either eliminated or supported by at least two fabrics of similar color, value, or style of print.

2. *If you can lose it, you can use it.* If you can fit a fabric somewhere in the range without it jumping out too obviously, go ahead and include it. Work hard to include—rather than exclude—a fabric by testing it in different spots with different neighbors. If you still can't lose it, it may not fit into your quilt—but don't make a final decision just yet. Remember that a few surprises will add interest, as long as they don't overwhelm the quilt.

Fabrics that typically cause problems are those with a high contrast between light and dark within the print, or between the motif and the background. Perhaps these fabrics will work when turned over, as the pattern may be softened when viewed from the reverse side. The difference may even be enough to push them from one category of fabric to another!

You may find you are able to use some parts of a fabric but not others. This is particularly so with large-scale print fabrics that contain expansive areas of solid-colored background. Pieces cut from the solid areas may not work in your quilt, while pieces cut from the printed areas may work very well.

Once you have sorted your fabrics into piles and completed your fabric runs, check the contrast at the margins of each run. Is your darkest light darker than your lightest dark? This does not necessarily mean you have to eliminate these fabrics, but you need to be careful in their placement, or perhaps shift them from one pile/run to another. The important thing is the contrast between the fabrics when they are placed side by side. When making blocks, make sure that the darkest lights are not placed next to the lightest darks, but rather with medium darks or darker darks. In some of our quilts, the same fabric was used as both a light and a dark, depending on its neighbors.

Sometimes, when there is minimal contrast between fabrics, the resultant blurring of the design adds interest. Again, it's a balance: a little blurring of the design in parts of the quilt may be good, but if there is too much blurring over the whole quilt, the pattern becomes lost.

CHOOSE A BLOCK PATTERN

HAVING CHOSEN your fabrics, the next step is to choose a block design to suit your fabric selection. Note the order here: it is best to work from the fabrics to the design rather than the other way around.

Experiment with several possibilities before choosing a block design. Look at the proportion of lights to darks within the various blocks you plan to try. If you have more dark fabrics, you will want to focus on designs that have more dark than light, and if you have more light fabrics, choose designs that have more light than dark. Cut some strips from a selection of your fabrics, and then crosscut them into rectangles (see pages 38–39). Cut enough rectangles to make at least four blocks.

Play with the rectangles on your design wall by arranging them into various block designs. Try several different arrangements until one "speaks" to you. Trust your eyes: the fabrics will usually tell you whether they are happy in the pattern or not. This playing is the most important step in helping you choose a pattern suitable for your fabrics. In a sense, you are customizing the design to work with your fabrics.

The six samples pictured below show the designs Judy tried before choosing one for "Two

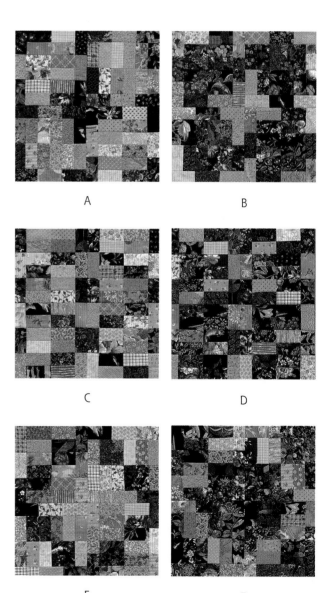

A

B

C

D

E

F

Experimenting with arrangements of light and dark fabrics

Yellow Canaries" (page 49). Since she had more dark than light fabrics, she liked Block F (lower right on page 17) best.

As you play with various arrangements of fabrics, remember to stand back and view the blocks at a distance to determine how well the pattern is coming through. Does the design still work, or is the pattern getting lost? Do any of the fabrics stand out too much?

We cannot stress enough the importance of this "play" in creating a successful quilt. It will not only help you choose the design, but it will also help you select fabrics.

At this playing stage, you may become aware of fabrics that are not working in your design. Or, the reverse may happen, as you realize a fabric you thought would not fit is just the one to give your quilt a lift. A fabric should add sparkle to the quilt, but not dominate or overwhelm the design. Test a questionable fabric by asking yourself if your eyes enjoy finding this piece, or if it jumps out so much that your eyes go nowhere else. If you really can't decide, leave the quilt for a while, preferably overnight, then look at it with fresh eyes later. If that fabric really still bothers you, you may need to eliminate it.

Once you have chosen your block design, it is a good idea to keep that arrangement of four blocks assembled on the design wall. That way, you can

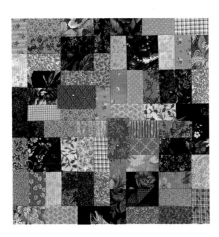

Auditioning questionable fabrics by pinning to four-block arrangement

cut a rectangle from a questionable fabric, and place it on top of one of your sample blocks to see how the fabric works in the design. These four blocks thus have a vital role in auditioning other fabrics as you proceed with your quilt.

ANALYZE THE BIG PICTURE

YOU HAVE made your fabric selection and chosen your block design. There are still a few important issues to consider in planning your quilt.

First, how big will the quilt be? Will it be a large bed quilt, or a small wall hanging or lap quilt? What size rectangle will you use? Predetermining size will help you decide how many blocks to make. Consider the overall quilt layout in making this decision, as some designs are more visually pleasing with an odd number of blocks while others look better with an even number (see "Finishing the Pattern" on page 28). In addition, some designs work best in a larger scale, especially those created from combinations of blocks.

Next, will you add borders, and if so, what kind? There are many possibilities here. You can add a border with strips of one fabric, or borders with two or more strips of varying widths. Alternatively, you may want more elaborately pieced borders, or you may want to complete the design by altering the basic blocks in some way. Options for pieced border designs are described on page 28.

It is sometimes best to postpone a final decision about borders until after you have finished the center of the quilt, especially if you want to add borders cut from long strips of fabric. You can then audition various fabrics to choose those that work best with the center of the quilt. Note that the border fabric does not need to be a fabric already used in the quilt.

Some quilts don't need borders and can be simply finished off with binding of suitable width.

THE DESIGNS

THE DESIGNS in this book were originally inspired by traditional arrangements of Japanese tatami mats. These mats are always made in exactly the same size, and their rectangular shape—the same size as two squares placed next to each other—allows them to be arranged in interlocking patterns. For example, two mats placed side by side form a larger square, three mats form a larger rectangle, and arrangements of both eight and eighteen mats make even larger squares. Since all the blocks are based on a single shape—the rectangle—all are one-patch designs.

Rectangle size is the same as two squares.

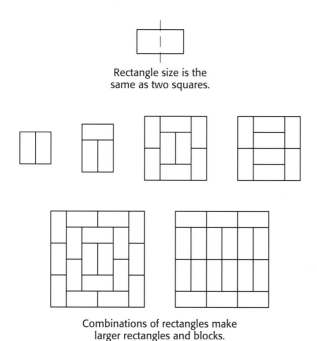

Combinations of rectangles make larger rectangles and blocks.

The combinations of rectangles come to life when some rectangles are dark and others light. There are many possibilities for making different block designs by varying the placement of darks and lights within each block.

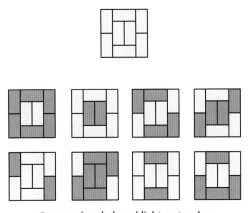

Rearranging dark and light rectangles yields different designs.

Blocks can then be repeated to make dramatic overall quilt designs. There are three different ways that patterns are created with repeating blocks.

1. By *repeating* the block without changing either the block itself or its orientation.

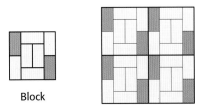

Block

Block repeated

2. By *reversing* the block, that is, making the block in a mirror image. Note that a block and its reverse are not the same and should not be confused with each other.

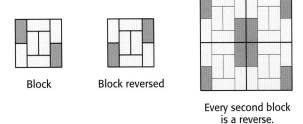

Block   Block reversed

Every second block is a reverse.

3. By *rotating* the block, or turning it from one of its corners. The block can be turned once (90 degrees or a quarter-turn), twice (180 degrees or a half-turn) or three times (270 degrees or a three-quarters turn). Think of these turns in terms of a clock face: you are turning a corner of the block to a three o'clock, six o'clock, or nine o'clock position.

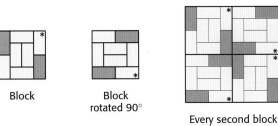

Block   Block rotated 90°

Every second block is rotated 90°.

Selecting Block Designs and Their Overall Patterns

WHAT FOLLOWS is a selection of some of our favorite block designs based on combinations of eight, eighteen, and three rectangles. We have numbered the designs for easy reference, numbering the eight-rectangle designs 8:1, 8:2, etc.; the eighteen-rectangle designs 18:1, 18:2, etc.; and the three-rectangle designs 3:1 and 3:2. We do not claim to have found every possible useful combination, so you may like to play the same design games we did by shading in squares on graph paper with a ¼" (5 mm) grid.

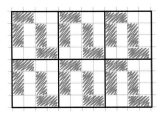

Use graph paper to experiment with block layouts.

The proportion of dark to light is very important when it comes to turning the designs into quilts. This proportion is useful to note when you assess your assembled fabrics. For example, if you have a lot of dark prints, you will want to make a predominantly dark quilt and therefore will choose a design with more darks than lights.

We have arbitrarily identified the blocks as "positive" and "negative" when the lights and darks appear in opposite positions.

EIGHT-RECTANGLE BLOCK DESIGNS

Design 8:1

Positive block

Negative block

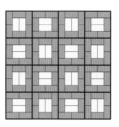

Positive blocks repeating, alternate blocks rotated 90°.

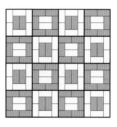

Negative and positive blocks alternating, positive blocks rotated 90°. See "Night and Day, Time Passing" (page 35) and "Spectrum" (page 69).

Design 8:2

Positive block

Reverse positive block

Negative block

Reverse negative block

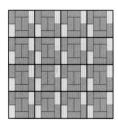

Positive blocks repeating. See "Cotton Candy" (page 31).

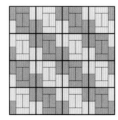

Positive and negative blocks alternating. See "Spring Song" (page 32).

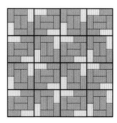

Positive blocks repeating, alternate blocks rotated 90°.

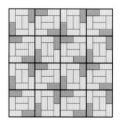

Negative blocks repeating, alternate blocks rotated 90°. See "Bondi Beach" (page 75).

Design 8:3

Positive block   Negative block

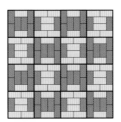

Negative blocks repeating, alternate blocks rotated 90°. See "Fashion Plate" (page 30).

Positive and negative blocks alternating, negative blocks rotated 90°.

Design 8:4

Positive block   Negative block   Reverse positive block   Reverse negative block

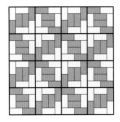 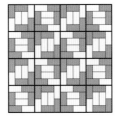 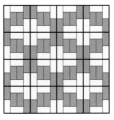 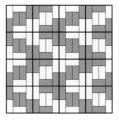

Positive blocks repeating, alternate blocks rotated 90°.

Negative blocks repeating, alternate blocks rotated 90°. See "An Old-Fashioned Quilt" (page 56).

Positive blocks, with alternate reverse (mirror-image) blocks.

Positive and negative blocks alternating, with reverse (mirror-image) blocks in alternate rows.

Design 8:5

Positive block   Negative block

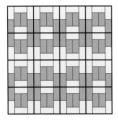 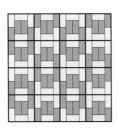 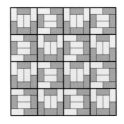 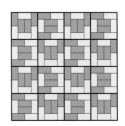

Positive blocks repeating, blocks rotated 180° in alternate rows.

Positive blocks repeating, alternate blocks rotated 180°.

Negative blocks repeating, alternate blocks rotated 90°. See "Lava Flow" (page 87).

Positive blocks repeating, alternate blocks rotated 90°.

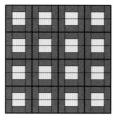
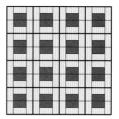

Positive block Negative block Positive blocks repeating. Negative blocks repeating.
See "Bento Box" (page 84).

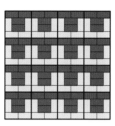
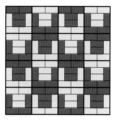

Positive block Negative block Positive blocks repeating. Positive and negative
blocks alternating.

Eighteen-Rectangle Block Designs

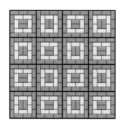
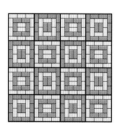

Positive block Negative block Positive blocks repeating, Negative and positive
alternate blocks rotated 90°. blocks alternating, positive
blocks rotated 90°. See
"Jewel Box" (page 29),
"The Alchemist's Furnace"
(page 33), and "Flush of
Spring" (page 59).

Positive block   Negative block

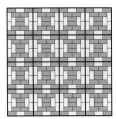

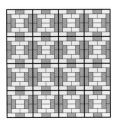

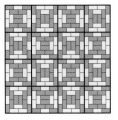

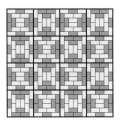

Positive blocks repeating.   Negative blocks repeating.   Positive blocks repeating, alternate blocks rotated 90°. See "Todd's Quilt" (page 34), "Left Out of Africa" (page 35), and "Indigo Weave" (page 72).   Negative blocks repeating, alternate blocks rotated 90°.

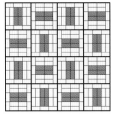

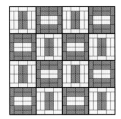

Positive block   Negative block   Negative blocks repeating, alternate blocks rotated 90°.   Negative and positive blocks alternating, positive blocks rotated 90°.

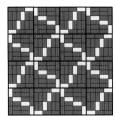

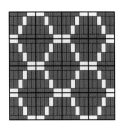

Block   Reverse block   Block repeating, alternate blocks rotated 90°. See "Down Memory Lane" (page 66).   Block and reverse block alternating.

Block

Reverse block

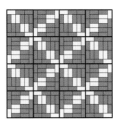

Block repeating, alternate blocks rotated 90°.

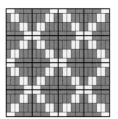

Block and reverse block alternating.

Positive block

Negative block

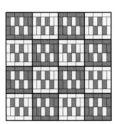

Positive and negative blocks alternating. See "Checkerboard" (page 78).

Positive block

Negative block

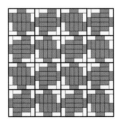

Positive blocks repeating, alternate blocks rotated 90°.

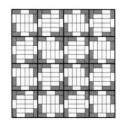

Negative blocks repeating, alternate blocks rotated 90°.

Eighteen-Rectangle Block Combinations

Block Combination 1

The easiest way to construct this pattern is to make the quilt in strips as shown.

Block 1

Block 2

Block 3

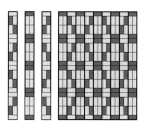

Three blocks repeating
with alternate block 3
rotated 180°.

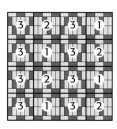

Piece in strips instead of blocks.

Block Combination 2

This pattern works best in a strong light/dark contrast. See "Something Blue" (page 30).

Block 1

Block 2

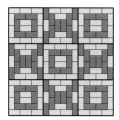

Block 1 and Block 2
alternating.

Three-Rectangle Block Designs

Design 3:1

See this arrangement in "Simply Scraps" (page 90).

Positive block

Negative block

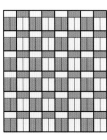

Positive and negative
blocks alternating.

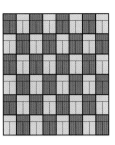

Positive block   Negative block   Positive and negative
blocks alternating.

USING THREE
OR MORE AREAS OF VALUE

MANY OF the previous designs can be made using three, or sometimes even more, areas of value. These values can be variations on the basic darks, mediums, and lights. Alternatively, different colors can create the areas of different value. In addition to the examples shown below, examples of quilts with three or more areas of value are "1-2-3 What Can You See?" (page 81) and "Christmas Lanterns" (page 93).

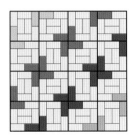

Block 8:2
See "Board Short Boogie-
Woogie" (page 31).

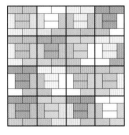

Block 8:7
See "Tee-Time" (page 32).

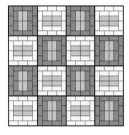

Block 18:3
See "Black and White and
Red All Over" (page 52).

Block 18:7
See "Van Gogh Stars"
(page 33) and "Autumn
Stars" (page 62).

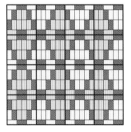

Block Combination 1
See "French Connections"
(page 34).

FINISHING THE PATTERN

OUR EYES read pattern from the outside in, so it is important to consider where a segment or unit of pattern begins and ends. Altering the blocks that fall along the edge of the design can make the overall result pleasingly complete. Alterations involve deleting elements of the design around the edges.

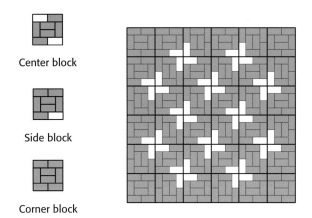

Center block

Side block

Corner block

This approach was used to visually complete the center of the design in quilts such as "Autumn Stars" (page 62) and "Bondi Beach" (page 75).

Some arrangements of blocks work best when there is an uneven number of blocks, as in the designs that repeat positive and negative blocks. This can be seen in quilts such as "Black and White and Red All Over" (page 52) and "Checkerboard" (page 78).

ADDING PIECED BORDERS

FOLLOWING ARE some ideas for border treatments using rectangles.

Three-rectangle units create the first option, with dark rectangles creating the outside edge. Note the all-dark unit used in the corners. This border treatment appears in "Two Yellow Canaries" (page 49) and "Down Memory Lane" (page 66).

Rectangles may be shaded from dark to light, as in "Jewel Box" (page 29) and "Van Gogh Stars" (page 33).

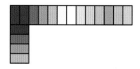

This border pairs rectangles with similar tonal value and appears in "Tee-Time" (page 32).

This combination of two different three-rectangle units looks like a threaded ribbon and can be seen in "Christmas Lanterns" (page 93).

You can design a block especially for a border, as seen in "Bondi Beach" (page 75).

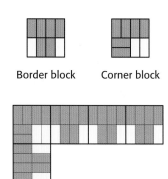

Border block   Corner block

You can also create the illusion of borders by shading blocks differently around the outside edges of a quilt. This border treatment appears in "Black and White and Red All Over" (page 52).

QUILT GALLERY

Jewel Box by Judy Turner, 46" x 61"
(117 cm x 155 cm). Block design 18:1 (page 23).

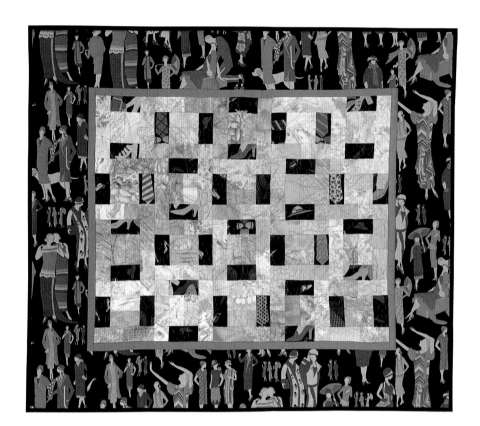

LEFT: **Fashion Plate** by Judy Turner, 36" x 41½" (91 cm x 105 cm). Machine quilted by Barbara Gower. Block design 8:3 (page 22).

RIGHT: **Something Blue** by Margaret Rolfe, 81" x 81" (206 cm x 206 cm). Block Combination 2 (page 26).

LEFT: **Board Short Boogie-Woogie** by Margaret Rolfe, 48" x 64" (122 cm x 162 cm). Machine quilted by Beth Reid. Block design 8:2 (page 21).

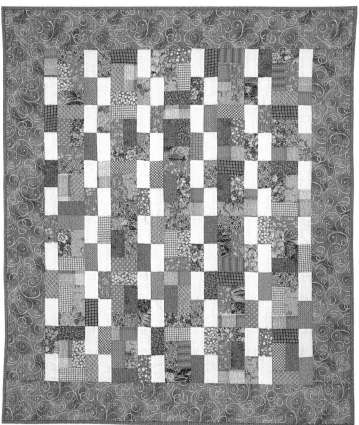

RIGHT: **Cotton Candy** by Margaret Rolfe, 40" x 44½" (102 cm x 113 cm). Machine quilted by Beth Reid. Block design 8:2 (page 21).

LEFT: **Spring Song** by Margaret Rolfe, 47½" x 59½" (121 cm x 151 cm). Machine quilted by Beth Reid. Block design 8:2 (page 21).

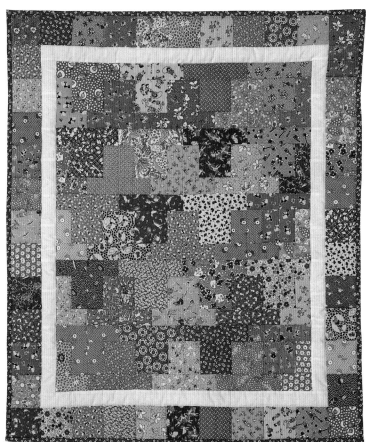

RIGHT: **Tee-Time** by Margaret Rolfe, 33" x 39" (84 cm x 100 cm). Block design 8:7 (page 23).

LEFT: **Van Gogh Stars** by Barbara Gower, 81" x 97½" (206 cm x 247 cm). Collection of Christopher Keen. Block design 18:7 (page 25).

RIGHT: **The Alchemist's Furnace** by Jenny Bowker, 63" x 72" (160 cm x 183 cm). Block design 18:1 (page 23).

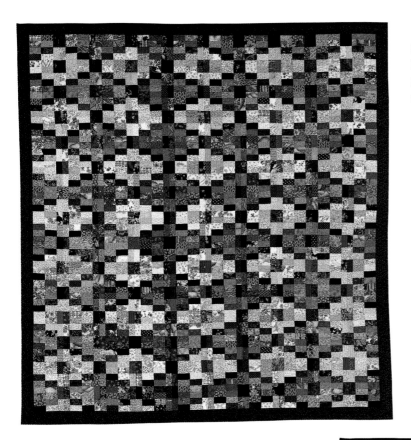

LEFT: **French Connections** by Libby Hepburn, 93" x 96" (236 cm x 244 cm). Machine quilted by Barbara Gower. Block Combination 1 (page 26).

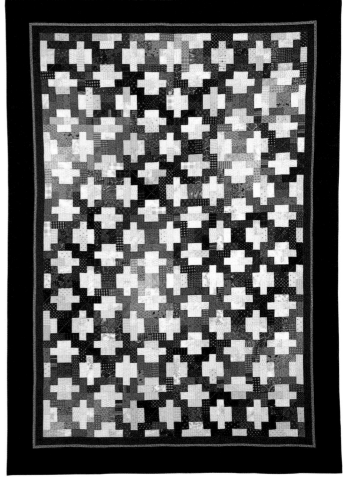

RIGHT: **Todd's Quilt** by Tracey Smith, 65½" x 90½" (166 cm x 230 cm). Machine quilted by Susan Campbell. Block design 18:2 (page 24).

LEFT: **Left Out of Africa** by Di Mansfield, 62" x 97" (157 cm x 246 cm). Block design 18:2 (page 24).

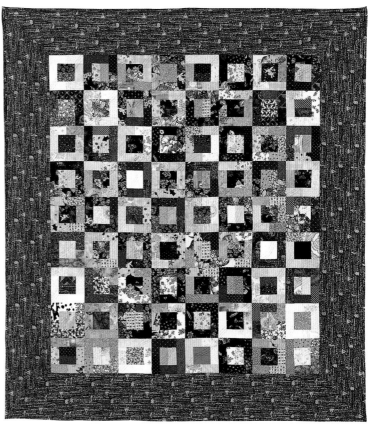

RIGHT: **Night and Day, Time Passing** by Karen Merchant, 64½" x 71" (164 cm x 180 cm). Block design 8:1 (page 21).

BLOCK ASSEMBLY

T
HE BLOCKS used to construct the quilts in this book use rectangles of two different sizes: 1½" x 3" (4 cm x 8 cm) or 2" x 4" (5 cm x 10 cm). *These are finished measurements;* that is, they indicate the size of the piece without seam allowances added, or the size you will see in the finished quilt. The rectangles must be cut to include ¼" (7.5 mm) seam allowances on all sides, so the smaller rectangles will be cut 2" x 3½" (5.5 cm x 9.5 cm), and the larger rectangles will be cut 2½" x 4½" (6.5 cm x 11.5 cm).

It is impossible to estimate precisely how much fabric you need when making a scrap quilt, because it is made from so many different pieces of fabric. Generally, the greater the variety, the better, with only small quantities used of each piece. Note that yardages for cutting rectangles (as shown in project instructions) are based on calculated approximations.

GATHERING MATERIALS AND EQUIPMENT

NOTE: *All measurements in this book are given in imperial (inches and yards) and metric (millimeters, centimeters, and meters) measurements. These measurements are not interchangeable; always use either one set or the other. The metric measurements are not exact equivalents, but measurements that are the nearest practical number. For example, 1" becomes 2.5 cm, 4" becomes 10 cm, and so on. All cutting measurements include seam allowances: ¼" for imperial measurements and 7.5 mm (0.75 cm) for metric measurements.*

Fabrics

Cotton fabrics, both in prints and solid colors, are the most suitable for quiltmaking. Cotton dress fabrics and decorator fabrics may also be used and can be a good source of larger-scaled prints, border prints, and patterns that are a "little bit different." However, avoid latex-backed fabrics.

We prefer to prewash and press fabrics before use, to avoid any possibility of shrinkage or color bleeding after the quilt is finished.

Batting

Batting choice is an individual matter. We have used all kinds of batting ourselves, including a polyester batting, which we like because it is light in weight and has good loft; a wool-and-polyester blend, because it is warm and comfortable to sleep under; and a cotton or cotton-and-polyester blend, which drapes well and can give a lovely flat, traditional look to quilts.

Threads

Use thread suitable for machine sewing when piecing by machine, choosing thread color to blend with the fabrics you are stitching. Neutrals make a good choice; gray is useful for dark quilts, and cream or ecru for light quilts.

For machine quilting, use a quality machine-sewing thread that suits the colors in the quilt top. Lay a long "squiggle" of thread across the quilt top to determine how the thread will look when sewn. Transparent nylon thread is an option when the quilting crosses fabrics of many colors, though it should only be used as the top thread and not in the bobbin.

For hand quilting, use specially designated hand-quilting thread, again choosing a color that suits the quilt.

Sewing Machine

Your sewing machine is your most vital tool for making scrap quilts. Accuracy in piecing is important if the pieces are to fit. The easiest and best way to maintain accuracy is to use a ¼" (7.5 mm) foot on your machine. This allows you to align the cut edge of the fabric with the edge of the foot so all seams finish exactly the same width. Consult your machine dealer; the accuracy obtained when using this foot is worth the purchase. Alternatively, some machines permit you to move the needle so that it is exactly ¼" (7.5 mm) from the edge of the foot. (Use a piece of graph paper as a guide.) Another possibility is to mark the throat plate of the machine with masking tape to indicate the exact width of the seam allowance. The cut edge of the fabric can then be aligned with this marking.

Love and look after your machine, as it will be your best friend through many pleasant hours of sewing. Clean lint away frequently, change needles regularly, and follow the manufacturer's directions to lubricate as necessary.

Rotary-Cutting Equipment

Rotary cutter: A medium-sized rotary cutter, with a blade 1¾" (4.5 cm) in diameter, is our preferred option. Replace blades whenever the cutter does not cut cleanly. Your back and wrist muscles will thank you for making their jobs easier! Always, and we repeat *always*, close the rotary cutter when not in use, even if only for the shortest time.

Mat: Choose a mat at least 12" x 18" (30 cm x 45 cm) for cutting smaller pieces of fabric, and a larger mat, at least 18" x 24" (45 cm x 60 cm), to cut long strips efficiently.

Rulers: You'll need a long rectangular acrylic ruler (e.g., 6" x 24", or 15 cm x 60 cm) for cutting long strips and borders, while a short rectangular ruler (e.g., 6" x 12", or 15 cm x 30 cm) is useful for cutting short strips and for crosscutting long strips into smaller pieces. A large square ruler (e.g., 12½" x 12½", or 32 cm x 32 cm) comes in handy for squaring up quilt corners and borders.

DESIGN WALL

A DESIGN wall allows you to view your work in progress and make the best visual choices for these quilts. Tape or pin a large piece of cotton flannel or batting to the wall, or—for a more permanent arrangement—use felt, cotton batting, or flannel to cover a sheet of foam core or other surface you can stick pins into.

VALUE-DETERMINING TOOLS

USE A reducing glass, or look through a camera lens or the wrong end of binoculars to view your work in progress. A door peephole, available in hardware and home-supply stores, makes another inexpensive alternative. These tools give the effect of looking at your work from a distance and help you determine how well the tonal values and colors are working over the surface of your quilt.

SEWING EQUIPMENT

Pins: Most of the blocks in this book will not require any pinning as you sew, although pins are useful as markers and also for securing some of the longer seams. Pins (and a wrist pincushion) are also useful for holding blocks on your design wall.

Needles: Size 80/12 sewing-machine needles are best for piecing and machine quilting typical cotton-quilting fabrics.

For hand-sewing tasks such as finishing the binding, choose any medium-sized hand-sewing needle that you find comfortable to thread and hold. Hand quilting requires a short needle, called a *between*.

Scissors: A small pair of scissors or thread snips are needed for trimming threads and so on.

Seam ripper: This tool is useful for the odd mistake, which inevitably occurs for all of us!

PRESSING EQUIPMENT

YOU'LL NEED an iron to press all seams. A steam iron (Judy's preference) or a spray bottle of water (Margaret's choice) helps in pressing the seams smooth and flat.

CUTTING RECTANGLES

THE RECTANGLE shape is ideal for rotary cutting, so cutting the pieces for these quilts is both easy and efficient.

NOTE: *All cutting instructions are for the right-handed quilter. Reverse if you are left-handed.*

Safety is an important issue when working with the sharp rotary-cutting tool. Remember always to close your rotary cutter when you are not using it, no matter how short a time. When cutting, keep fingers firmly on top of the ruler, away from the sharp blade. And finally, never leave the rotary cutter where a child might find it.

The first step for all rotary cutting is to establish a straight edge from which measurements can be made. When working with small pieces or scraps of fabric, place the fabric on your cutting mat and cut down the right-hand edge of the fabric. Turn

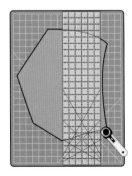 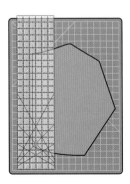

the fabric so the cut edge is now to your left, and you are ready for cutting strips.

To cut large pieces of fabric, fold the fabric selvage to selvage, shaking it gently to remove wrinkles and creases. Place the folded fabric on your cutting mat, with the fold directly in front of you. Place the ruler on the right-hand side of the fabric, matching the base of the ruler exactly with the fold. (Make sure the ruler is at an exact right angle to the fold, or when you unfold the fabric, you will find you have cut a V-shaped strip!) Trim the fabric edge. Without moving the fabric, rotate the cutting mat so that the cut edge is now to your left, ready for cutting strips.

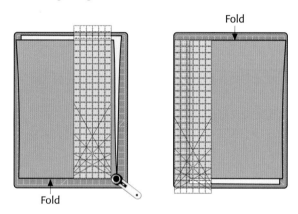

To cut individual rectangles from small scraps of fabric, use your rotary cutter to cut two sides of the rectangle. Turn the fabric, replace the ruler to measure the exact size of the rectangle desired, and cut the remaining two sides.

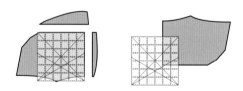

Use the following method to cut rectangles from strips:

1. After straightening the edge of the fabric as described at left, use your ruler to measure and cut strips of the desired width. The strips can be cut either the width or the length of the rectangle (including seam allowance), depending upon which makes the most economical use of your piece of fabric.

2. After trimming one end of the strip to straighten it, use your ruler to measure and crosscut the strip into the desired number of rectangles.

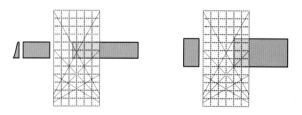

CUTTING EFFICIENTLY

JUDY LIKES to cut rectangles in multiples to make the job of cutting as quick and efficient as possible. *Work carefully for accurate results.*

1. Cut fabric strips designated for rectangles to approximately 21" (56 cm) long. Lay the strips parallel to each other on a large mat, overlapping the strips slightly. Use the grid on your mat to make sure the strips are lined up perfectly.

2. Use a long ruler to trim and straighten the right edge of the parallel strips. Position the ruler carefully, so as not to disturb the laid-out strips. Again being careful not to disturb the strips, turn the mat so that the trimmed edge is to your left.

3. Use your ruler to measure and crosscut the parallel strips into rectangles of the desired length. Again, take care when cutting and repositioning the ruler so as not to disturb the layout of strips.

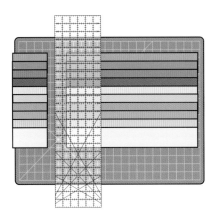

SEWING RECTANGLES

IT IS essential that you maintain an accurate ¼" (7.5 mm) seam allowance when sewing the rectangles together. Always check before beginning to sew.

Place two rectangles right sides together, aligning the long raw edges. Sew and press the seam to one side. Place a third rectangle lengthwise above the two joined rectangles as shown, and compare. The width of the two sewn rectangles should exactly match the length of the third rectangle. If it does not, continue trying until you get an exact match, indicating that your seam allowance is a perfect ¼" (7.5 mm).

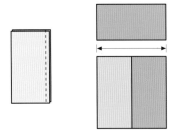

CHAIN PIECING

WHENEVER POSSIBLE, chain-piece rectangles together to save time and thread.

1. Sew the first pair of rectangles from cut edge to cut edge. At the end of the seam, stop sewing, but do not cut the thread.

2. Feed the next pair of rectangles under the presser foot, as close as possible to the first pair. Continue feeding pieces through the machine without cutting the threads in between. You do not need to backstitch.

3. When all pieces have been sewn, remove the chain from the machine, and clip the thread between the pairs.

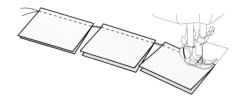

CONSTRUCTING THE BLOCKS

THERE ARE two methods for constructing blocks. The method you choose will depend upon the arrangement of the individual rectangles within the block. The suggested construction method for each block is included in the project instructions.

BLOCKS WITH CENTER-TO-OUTSIDE CONSTRUCTION

THE RECTANGLES in these blocks are arranged so that the pieces cannot be assembled in rows, but rather are built in units from the center outward. First, lay out the entire block. Beginning with the center of the block, assemble the various units, and join them until the block is complete. Press seam allowances to one side after sewing each seam.

  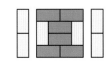

BLOCKS WITH THREE-RECTANGLE-UNIT CONSTRUCTION

THESE BLOCKS are easiest to construct in three-rectangle units.

Lay out the units for each block before sewing the block together. This enables you to check that you are not using a fabric twice within the block. It also allows you to note which units are next to each other and, whenever possible, to press adjacent seams in opposite directions so the seam allowances interlock and the block lies flat. (Whenever practical, illustrations for the projects in this book include pressing arrows to help you with this step.) Then you can proceed to sew the units together to make the block.

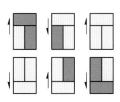

It will not always be possible to make all seam allowances interlock, so accept that sometimes seams will need to be pressed in the same direction.

QUILT CONSTRUCTION

ALWAYS LAY out the completed blocks before sewing them together. This is your last opportunity to make sure that colors and values are distributed as you wish throughout the quilt. Accent colors should be scattered over the quilt and not clumped together. To help in this process, look at the quilt through a reducing glass or camera lens.

JOINING THE BLOCKS

THERE ARE two methods of joining the blocks to make the quilt center: joining the blocks into horizontal rows first, which Margaret prefers; or joining the blocks into vertical rows first, which Judy prefers.

JOINING THE BLOCKS IN HORIZONTAL ROWS

1. Write the row number for each horizontal row on a small slip of paper, and pin the label to the first (left) block in the row. Place the pins horizontally, with the pins pointed in opposite directions from row to row. The direction of the pins will indicate the direction to press the seams.

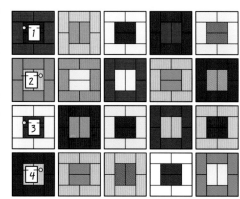

2. Beginning from the left, stack the blocks in each horizontal row, keeping them in order, with the labeled block on top. Be careful not to change the orientation of the blocks.

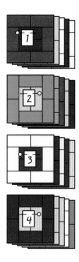

3. Sew the blocks together into horizontal rows, pressing the seams in the direction indicated by the point of the pin.

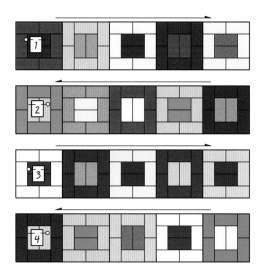

4. Sew the rows together to make the quilt. Reduce the bulk when sewing a large quilt by constructing the quilt in two halves, then sewing the two halves together. Press the seams to one side.

JOINING THE BLOCKS IN VERTICAL ROWS

1. Write the row number for each vertical row on a small slip of paper, and pin the label to the first (top) block in the row.

2. Beginning from the top, stack the blocks in each vertical row, keeping them in order, with the labeled block on top. Be careful not to change the orientation of the blocks.

3. Take the piles of row 1 and row 2 blocks to your sewing machine. Sew the top block from row 1 to the top block from row 2. Repeat to sew the second block from row 1 to the second block from row 2, and so on, until all row 1 and row 2 blocks are joined in pairs. Do not snip the thread between pairs of blocks, and do not press the seams yet. When you have finished, the two vertical rows will be joined, with one long vertical thread.

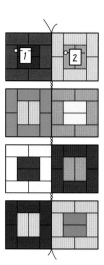

4. Take the pile of row 3 blocks to the machine and repeat step 3 to sew the row 3 blocks to the row 2 blocks. Continue adding rows until all vertical rows are joined. The blocks will all be joined together along their vertical seams, but no horizontal seams will be sewn. Press the seams in opposite directions from row to row.

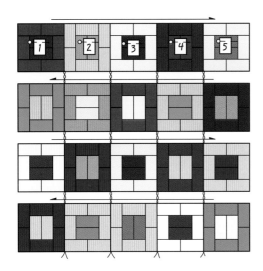

5. Sew the horizontal seams to complete the quilt center. Press the seams to one side.

ADDING THE BORDERS

BORDERS CAN be added as whole strips of fabric, or they can be pieced from rectangles or additional blocks (see page 28).

BORDER STRIPS WITH BUTTED CORNERS

NOTE: *For a flat quilt with straight edges, always measure your quilt top through its vertical and horizontal center.*

1. For the side borders, cut two strips a little longer (about 1" or 2.5 cm) than the length of the quilt top. For the top and bottom borders, cut two strips a little longer than the width of the quilt top plus the width of the two side borders. If you are piecing strips together, make the joins as invisible as possible by matching the design of the print and by pressing the seams open.

2. Lay the quilt top flat. Place the two strips for the side borders lengthwise down the center of the quilt top as shown. The border strips will be slightly longer than the quilt top. Pin-mark the ends of the border strips parallel to the edges of the quilt.

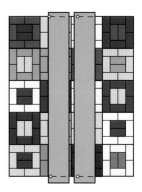

Lay borders over center of top.
Place pins to mark the quilt top edges.

3. Fold each side border strip in half and pin-mark the center. Fold the quilt top in half and pin-mark the center at each side. For a large quilt, fold both the border strips and quilt top once again to pin-mark in quarters.

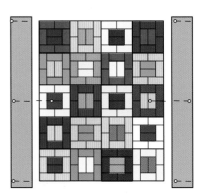

4. Matching pin marks, generously pin the borders to the quilt. Sew the borders to the quilt, and press seams toward the borders. Use your rotary cutter and a square ruler to square the borders even with the edges of the quilt top.

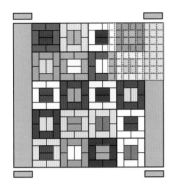

5. Lay the quilt top out flat. Place the top and bottom borders across the center of the quilt top as shown. Pin-mark the border strips parallel to the edges of the quilt sides.

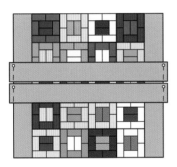

6. Fold and pin-mark the quilt top and top and bottom border strips as in step 3, this time folding across the width of the quilt top.

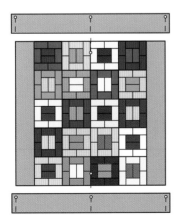

7. Repeat step 4 to pin, sew, and trim the borders.

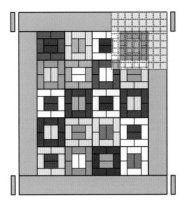

8. Repeat steps 1–7 as needed to attach any additional borders.

Border Strips with Mitered Corners

Note: *If the quilt has multiple borders, join the strips together into border units before proceeding.*

1. Measure the quilt top through its horizontal and vertical center. Cut two border strips to each measurement, plus double the width of the border and an extra 1" (2.5 cm). Pin-mark the midpoint of all four edges of the quilt top. Also pin-mark the midpoint of each border strip, and the point at which the border should match the edge of the quilt top.

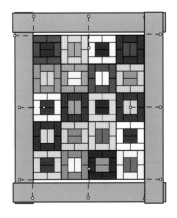

2. Pin the borders to the quilt top, carefully matching pin marks. Stitch the borders to the quilt, stopping and starting with a backstitch ¼" (7.5 mm) from the raw edges of the quilt top. Press the seams toward the borders.

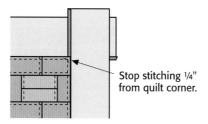

Stop stitching ¼" from quilt corner.

3. Working one corner at a time, place adjacent borders right sides together, aligning the long raw edges. Use a ruler and pencil to mark a 45-degree angle from the corner where you stopped stitching to the outside edge of the border.

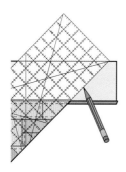

4. Pin the borders together, carefully matching any stripes or seams. Sew along the marked line, and trim away the excess border fabric, leaving a ¼" (7.5 mm) -wide seam allowance. Press these seams open.

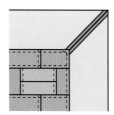

PIECED BORDERS

SINCE PIECED borders are made from the same rectangles as the blocks and block units, they should fit perfectly, but it is always a good idea to check before you begin sewing them to the quilt top. If the pieced borders are too long, take them in by increasing the width of some or all of the seams. If, conversely, the pieced borders are too short, unpick and resew some or all of the seams so they are slightly smaller.

In most cases, pieced borders are sewn to the sides of the quilt first, then to the top and bottom of the quilt. This order may be varied, however, for a particular design to work.

LAYERING THE QUILT

IDEALLY, THE backing and batting should measure approximately 4" (10 cm) larger than the length and width of the finished quilt top. If necessary, divide the backing fabric crosswise (selvage to selvage), remove the selvage, and sew the panels together along the lengthwise edge to make one large backing piece. Press the joining seams open. You can orient the seam in whatever direction makes the most economical use of the fabric.

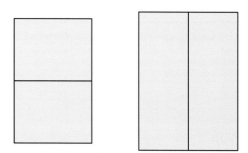

1. Spread the backing, wrong side up, over a large, clean, flat surface, smoothing out any wrinkles. Center and smooth the batting and then the well-pressed quilt top over the backing.

2. If you plan to machine quilt, baste all three layers thoroughly by fastening safety pins approximately every 3" to 4" (8 cm to 10 cm). Think carefully about where you plan to quilt so that you can place pins out of the path of quilting lines. If you plan to hand quilt, baste with thread instead of pins. Stitch vertical and horizontal lines to create a 3" to 4" (8 cm to 10 cm) grid across the quilt.

QUILTING

THESE PIECED quilts are very easy to quilt by machine, although you can hand quilt if you prefer. Easy patterns include grids of straight lines (horizontal, vertical, diagonal, or any combination), which can often be quilted across the quilt by following the piecing. If necessary, you can continue lines across unpieced borders by marking them with a chalk marker or other preferred marking tool. Other easy options include grids of wavy lines and meandering lines (done with a darning foot, feed dogs down, and free-motion stitching).

> Try to keep a large, clear space to the left of your machine to support the quilt as you maneuver it under the machine's arm. A flatbed setup is ideal, especially for free-motion stitching.

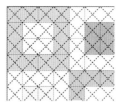
Straight-line grid

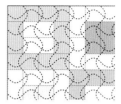
Meandering-line grid

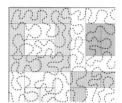
Free-motion stitching

BINDING THE QUILT

1. Trim the batting and backing of the quilt so approximately ⅛" to ¼" (5 mm to 7.5 mm) extends beyond the quilt top to fill the binding. Leave a bit more if the binding is extra wide.

2. Cut straight-grain strips in the width indicated in the project instructions. Measure the quilt through its center. Referring to the project instructions for the width, cut two strips a little longer than the length of the quilt (about 1", or 2.5 cm) for the side binding strips, and two strips a little longer than the width of the quilt for the top and bottom binding strips. If needed, join strips to make the lengths required, and press the seams open.

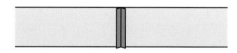

3. Fold the strips in half lengthwise, wrong side together, and press.

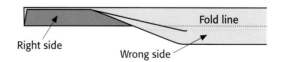
Fold line
Right side
Wrong side

4. Place the two side binding strips lengthwise down the center of the quilt. Pin-mark the ends of the strips parallel to the edges of the quilt. Fold each side binding strip in half and pin-mark the center. Pin-mark the midpoint of the sides of the quilt. With right sides together and matching pin marks on the binding strips and quilt, pin the binding to the quilt. Sew the binding to the quilt and trim the ends. Fold the binding to the back of the quilt and pin.

5. Place the top and bottom binding strips across the center of the quilt. Pin-mark the ends of the strips parallel to the edges of the quilt. Fold and pin-mark the midpoint of the binding strips and pin-mark the midpoint of the top and bottom edges of the quilt. Pin and sew the binding strips to the quilt. Fold the binding to the back of the quilt and pin.

6. Use matching thread to hand stitch the binding to the back of the quilt. Trim, fold, and stitch the excess binding at the corners so the corners are neat and square.

ADDING FINISHING TOUCHES

1. Add a sleeve to the back of any quilt that will hang on the wall. From backing fabric, cut a strip about 8" (20 cm) wide by the width of the quilt. Hem both short ends of the strip with a double ¼" (7.5 mm) -wide hem. Fold the strip in half lengthwise, right sides together, and stitch. Turn right side out and press. Use matching thread to hand stitch the sleeve in place.

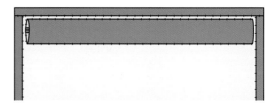

2. Stitch a label to the back of the quilt, giving your name, the date, and any other information, such as the quilt title, a special personal inscription, your address, the quilt's size, or the kind of batting used. Labels may be written on a square of fabric in permanent-ink pen, or embroidered by hand or machine.

Simply Scraps
by Judy Turner
2001

TWO YELLOW CANARIES

BY JUDY TURNER

JUDY HAS ALWAYS *loved the combination of black and pink. For years, she has collected prints with black (or navy) backgrounds and splashy multicolored prints. Prints in "Two Yellow Canaries" include floral, geometric, paisley, novelty, and animal patterns. Although the color scheme is basically black and pink, the dark prints featuring yellow play an important role in the quilt, so Judy cut extra pieces to work with. No tone-on-tone black fabrics are used; all are dark and multicolored. The pink fabrics are more subdued and do include lots of pink tone-on-tones.*

FINISHED QUILT SIZE:
63" x 81" (168 cm x 216 cm)

FINISHED BLOCK SIZE:
9" (24 cm) square

BLOCK DESIGN: 18:5

MATERIALS

44" (112 cm) -wide fabric
- 4¼ yds. (4.3 m) *total* of assorted black and navy multicolored prints for blocks and border
- 2 yds. (2 m) *total* of assorted pink prints for blocks and border
- ⅔ yd. (60 cm) black print for binding
- 4¼ yds. (4.6 m) print for backing
- 67" x 85" (178 cm x 226 cm) piece of batting

CUTTING

All measurements include ¼" (7.5 mm) -wide seam allowances. Cut binding strips from width of fabric.

From the assorted black and navy multicolored prints, cut a *total* of:
- 784 rectangles, each 2" x 3½" (5.5 cm x 9.5 cm), for blocks and border

From the assorted pink prints, cut a *total* of:
- 350 rectangles, each 2" x 3½" (5.5 cm x 9.5 cm), for blocks and border

From the black print, cut:
- 8 strips, each 2½" (6.5 cm) wide, for binding

MAKING THE BLOCKS

YOU'LL NEED a total of 48 pieced blocks for this quilt. Avoid duplicating fabrics in the units and blocks.

1. Sew the black and navy multicolored print rectangles and pink print rectangles to make the units shown. Press the seams for units A and B as indicated by the arrows. Units C and D will be pressed later. Make 88 of unit A, 88 of unit B, 116 of unit C, and 86 of unit D. Set 4 of unit C and all of unit D aside for the border.

Unit A
Make 88.

Unit B
Make 88.

Unit C
Make 116.

Unit D
Make 86.

2. For block 1, arrange units A, B, and C in 2 rows as shown. Sew the units into rows. Press the seams as indicated by the arrows. Sew the rows together to complete the block; press. Make 44 of block 1.

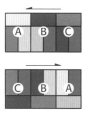

Block 1
Make 44.

3. For block 2, arrange 6 of unit C in 2 rows as shown. Sew and press as for block 1. Make 4 of block 2.

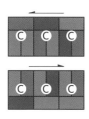

Block 2
Make 4.

ASSEMBLING THE QUILT

1. Refer to the quilt assembly diagram at right. Arrange the blocks in 8 horizontal rows of 6 blocks each, making sure to place a block 2 unit in each corner. Rotate alternate blocks within each row and from row to row as shown.

2. Sew the blocks together into rows. Press the seams in opposite directions from row to row.

3. Pin and sew the rows together; press.

4. Arrange 24 of unit D in a row to make a side border unit as shown. Press the top seam in opposite directions from unit to unit. Sew the units together and press the seams to one side. Make 2 border units.

Make 2 side borders.

5. Arrange 2 of unit C and 19 of unit D in a row to make a top/bottom border unit as shown. Press the top seam in opposite directions from unit to unit. Sew the units together and press the seams to one side. Make 2 border units.

Make a top and a bottom border.

6. Sew border units from step 4 to the sides of the quilt top. Press the seams toward the border units. Repeat to sew border units from step 5 to the top and bottom of the quilt top; press.

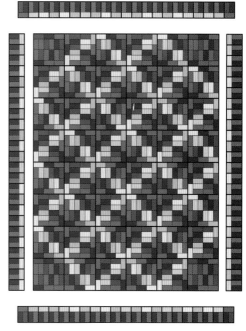

Assembly Diagram

FINISHING

1. Divide the backing fabric crosswise into 2 equal panels of approximately 85" (230 cm) each. Join the panels to make a single large backing panel.

2. Center and layer the quilt top and batting over the backing; baste.

3. Quilt as desired.

4. Use the 2½" (6.5 cm) -wide binding strips to make the binding. Sew the binding to the quilt.

BLACK AND WHITE AND RED ALL OVER

BY JUDY TURNER. MACHINE QUILTED BY BARBARA GOWER.

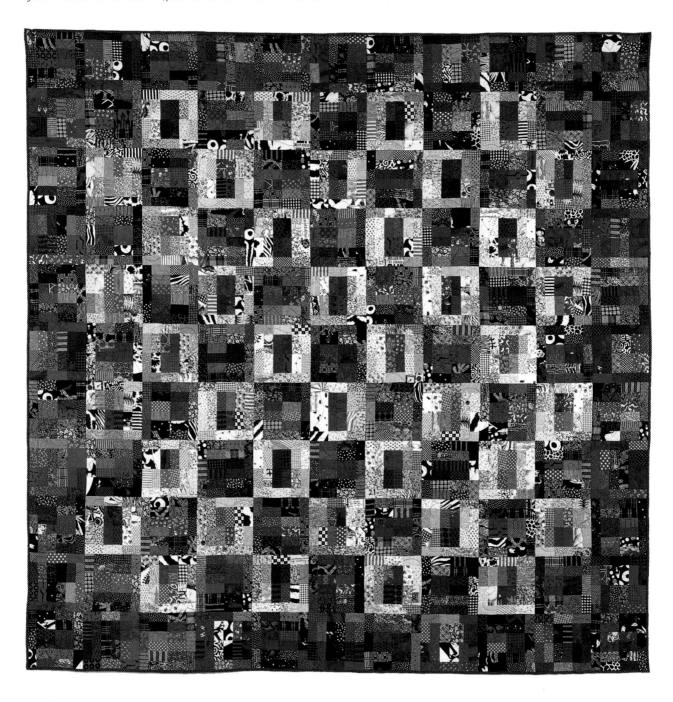

J UDY AIMED FOR *a contemporary look with this quilt. The fabrics include prints from the last three decades along with some prints commemorating the year 2000, the year the quilt was made. The prints include spots, stripes, checks, reproduction '30s prints, florals, tone-on-tones, Christmas prints, Japanese prints, batiks, African prints, and novelty prints. The border of the quilt is created simply by changing the colorway of alternate blocks in the outside row.*

FINISHED QUILT SIZE:
99" x 99" (264 cm x 264 cm)

FINISHED BLOCK SIZE:
9" (24 cm) square

BLOCK DESIGN: 18:3

MATERIALS

44" (112 cm) -wide fabric

- 3 yds. (3.2 m) *total* of assorted black–and–white prints with white predominant, for blocks
- 5 yds. (5.2 m) *total* of assorted black–and–white prints with black predominant, for blocks and border
- 3¾ yds. (3.8 m) *total* of assorted red prints for blocks and border
- ¾ yd. (80 cm) black print for binding
- 8¾ yds. (8.3 m) print for backing
- 103" x 103" (274 cm x 274 cm) piece of batting

CUTTING

All measurements include ¼" (7.5 mm) -wide seam allowances. Cut binding strips from width of fabric.

From the assorted black-and-white prints (white predominant), cut a *total* of:
- 560 rectangles, each 2" x 3½" (5.5 cm x 9.5 cm), for blocks

From the assorted black-and-white prints (black predominant), cut a *total* of:
- 934 rectangles, each 2" x 3½" (5.5 cm x 9.5 cm), for blocks and border

From the assorted red prints, cut a *total* of:
- 684 rectangles, each 2" x 3½" (5.5 cm x 9.5 cm), for blocks and border

From the black print, cut:
- 10 strips (11 for metric), each 2½" (6.5 cm) wide, for binding

MAKING THE BLOCKS

YOU'LL NEED a total of 121 pieced blocks for this quilt. Avoid duplicating prints in the units and blocks.

1. Sew the black-and-white print (white predominant) rectangles, black-and-white print (black predominant) rectangles, and red print rectangles to make the units shown. Press the seams as indicated by the arrows. Make 160 of unit A, 244 of unit B, 122 of unit C, 80 of unit D, 40 of unit E, and 80 of unit F.

Unit A
Make 160.

Unit B
Make 244.

Unit C
Make 122.

Unit D
Make 80.

Unit E
Make 40.

Unit F
Make 80.

2. For block 1, arrange units B and C in 2 rows as shown. Sew the units into rows. Press the seams as indicated by the arrows. Sew the rows together to complete the block; press. Make 61 of block 1.

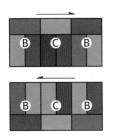
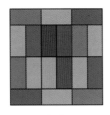

Block 1
Make 61.

3. For block 2, arrange units A and F in 2 rows as shown. Sew and press as for block 1. Make 40 of block 2.

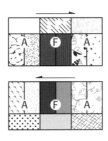
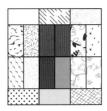

Block 2
Make 40.

4. For block 3, arrange units D and E in 2 rows as shown. Sew and press as for block 1. Make 20 of block 3.

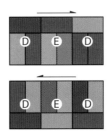
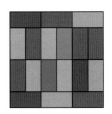

Block 3
Make 20.

Note range of values used in the black, white, and red areas of the blocks.

ASSEMBLING THE QUILT

1. Refer to the quilt assembly diagram below. Arrange the blocks in 11 horizontal rows of 11 blocks each, making sure to alternate and to rotate the blocks as shown. The illusion of a border is created by alternating block 1 and block 3 units.

2. Sew the blocks together into rows. Press the seams in opposite directions from row to row.

3. Pin and sew the rows together; press.

FINISHING

1. Divide the backing fabric crosswise into 3 equal panels of approximately 105" (274 cm) each. Join the panels to make a single large backing panel.

2. Center and layer the quilt top and batting over the backing; baste.

3. Quilt as desired.

4. Use the 2½" (6.5 cm) -wide binding strips to make the binding. Sew the binding to the quilt.

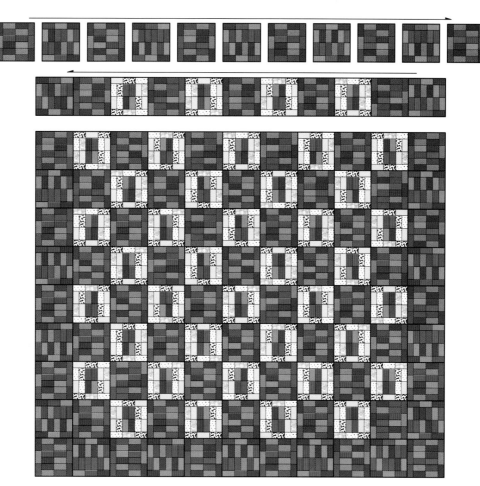

Assembly Diagram

An Old-Fashioned Quilt

BY MARGARET ROLFE

MARGARET IS A *quilt historian and loves old quilts. She particularly enjoys the many reproduction fabrics being made at the moment, and this particular quilt was built around her collection of Civil War–era reproduction fabrics. The red prints provide the accent, adding warmth and sparkle.*

FINISHED QUILT SIZE:
60" x 72" (160 cm x 192 cm)

FINISHED BLOCK SIZE:
6" (16 cm) square

BLOCK DESIGN: 8:4

MATERIALS

44" (112 cm) -wide fabric

- 1¾ yds. (1.8 m) *total* of assorted dark prints in various colors for blocks
- 1¾ yds. (1.8 m) *total* of assorted light prints (e.g., beige and light pink) for blocks
- 1¾ yds. (1.7 m) brown print for border and binding
- 3¾ yds. (3.4 m) print for backing
- 64" x 76" (170 cm x 202 cm) piece of batting

CUTTING

All measurements include ¼" (7.5 mm) -wide seam allowances. Cut border and binding strips along the length of fabric (parallel to selvage).

From the assorted dark prints, cut a *total* of:

- 320 rectangles, each 2" x 3½" (5.5 cm x 9.5 cm), for blocks

From the assorted light prints, cut a *total* of:

- 320 rectangles, each 2" x 3½" (5.5 cm x 9.5 cm), for blocks

From the brown print, cut:
- 4 strips, each 6½" (17.5 cm) wide, for border
- 5 strips, each 2½" (6.5 cm) wide, for binding

MAKING THE BLOCKS

YOU'LL NEED a total of 80 pieced blocks for this quilt. Avoid duplicating prints within the blocks.

Arrange 4 dark print and 4 light print rectangles as shown. Sew the rectangles together; press. Make 80 blocks.

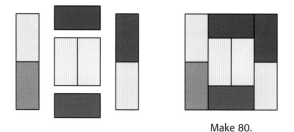

Make 80.

ASSEMBLING THE QUILT

1. Refer to the quilt assembly diagram below. Arrange the blocks in 10 horizontal rows of 8 blocks each. Make sure to scatter any accent prints over the quilt. Rotate alternate blocks within each row and from row to row as shown.

2. Sew the blocks together into rows. Press the seams in opposite directions from row to row.

3. Pin and sew the rows together; press.

4. Refer to "Border Strips with Butted Corners" (page 44) to fit and sew the 6½" (17.5 cm) -wide brown print border strips to the quilt.

FINISHING

1. Divide the backing fabric crosswise into 2 equal panels of approximately 67" (170 cm) each. Join the panels to make a single large backing panel.

2. Center and layer the quilt top and batting over the backing; baste.

3. Quilt as desired.

4. Use the 2½" (6.5 cm) -wide binding strips to make the binding. Sew the binding to the quilt.

Assembly Diagram

FLUSH OF SPRING

BY JUDY TURNER

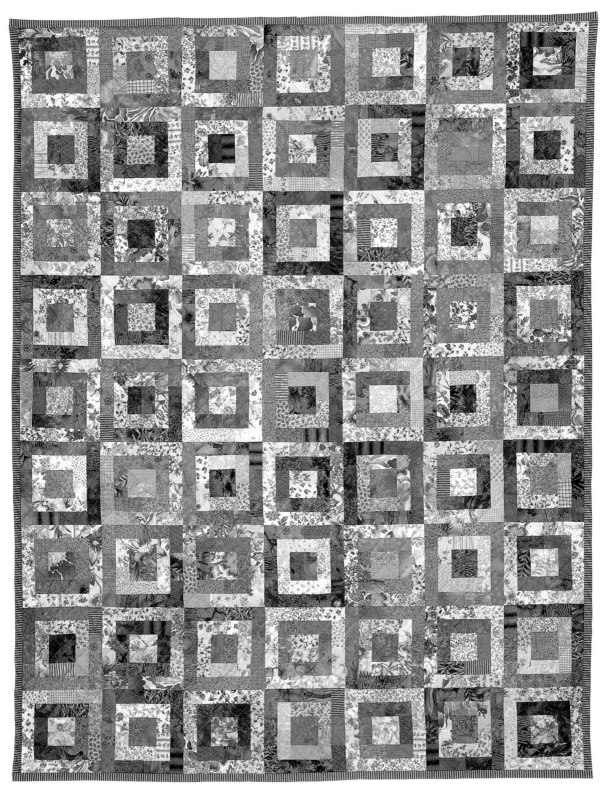

How welcome the *spring blossoms are after the cold winter! In this quilt, Judy uses a wide variety of green and pink prints to represent the season, blending the colors around the successive squares in each block. A wide binding of green edges the quilt.*

FINISHED QUILT SIZE:
63" x 81" (168 cm x 216 cm)

FINISHED BLOCK SIZE:
9" (24 cm) square

BLOCK DESIGN: 18:1

MATERIALS

44" (112 cm) -wide fabric
- 3 yds. (3.2 m) *total* of assorted light pink prints for blocks
- 3 yds. (3.2 m) *total* of assorted green prints for blocks
- 1¼ yds. (1 m) green striped fabric for binding
- 4¾ yds. (4.6 m) print for backing
- 67" x 85" (178 cm x 226 cm) piece of batting

CUTTING

All measurements include ¼" (7.5 mm) -wide seam allowances. Cut binding strips from width of fabric.

From the assorted light pink prints, cut a *total* of:
- 570 rectangles, each 2" x 3½" (5.5 cm x 9.5 cm), for blocks

From the assorted green prints, cut a *total* of:
- 564 rectangles, each 2" x 3½" (5.5 cm x 9.5 cm), for blocks

From the green striped fabric, cut:
- 8 strips, each 4½" (11.5 cm) wide, for binding

MAKING THE BLOCKS

YOU'LL NEED a total of 63 pieced blocks for this quilt. Avoid duplicating prints within the block.

1. For block 1, arrange 12 light pink print and 6 green print rectangles as shown. Blend the colors through the pink and green areas of each block (see "Blending" on page 14). Sew the rectangles together; press. Make 32 of block 1.

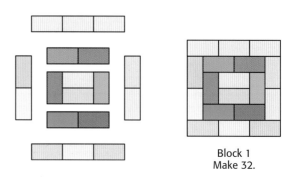

Block 1
Make 32.

2. For block 2, arrange 12 green print and 6 light pink print rectangles as shown. Blend the colors through the pink and green areas of each block. Sew the rectangles together; press. Make 31 of block 2.

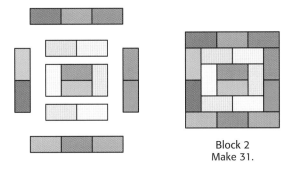

Block 2
Make 31.

ASSEMBLING THE QUILT

1. Refer to the quilt assembly diagram at right. Arrange the blocks in 9 horizontal rows of 7 blocks each, making sure to rotate alternate (block 2) blocks as shown.

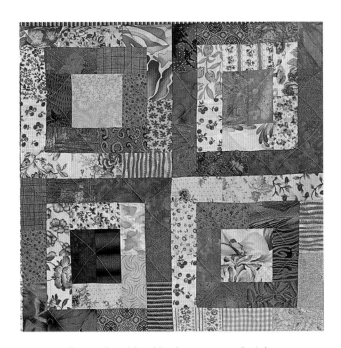

Note how colors blend in the green and pink areas.

2. Sew the blocks together into rows. Press the seams in opposite directions from row to row.

3. Pin and sew the rows together; press.

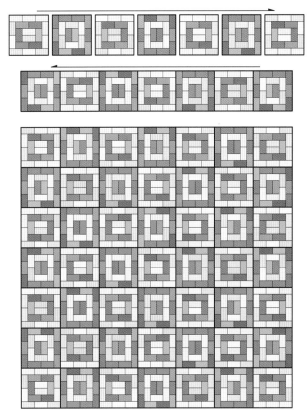

Assembly Diagram

FINISHING

1. Divide the backing fabric crosswise into 2 equal panels of approximately 85" (230 cm) each. Join the panels to make a single large backing panel.

2. Center and layer the quilt top and batting over the backing; baste.

3. Quilt as desired.

4. Use the 4½" (11.5 cm) -wide binding strips to make the binding. Sew the binding to the quilt.

AUTUMN STARS

BY JUDY TURNER

A utumn is particularly *beautiful in Canberra, where both Judy and Margaret live, and the season's rich range of colors provided wonderful inspiration for this quilt. Multicolored prints in autumn tones create the dark areas of the design, while flashes of blue provide an important color accent. Two values of beige prints define the starlike shapes in the corners between the blocks.*

FINISHED QUILT SIZE:
54" x 72" (144 cm x 192 cm)

FINISHED BLOCK SIZE:
9" (24 cm) square

BLOCK DESIGN: 18:7

MATERIALS

44" (112 cm) -wide fabric
- 3½ yds. (3.7 m) *total* of assorted dark autumn-toned multicolored prints for blocks and border
- ½ yd. (40 cm) *total* of assorted dark beige prints for blocks and border
- ¾ yd. (80 cm) *total* of assorted light beige prints for blocks and border
- ⅝ yd. (50 cm) rust print for binding
- 3¼ yds. (3.1 m) print for backing
- 58" x 76" (154 cm x 202 cm) piece of batting

CUTTING

All measurements include ¼" (7.5 mm) -wide seam allowances. Cut binding strips from width of fabric.

From the assorted dark autumn-toned multicolored prints, cut a *total* of:
- 652 rectangles, each 2" x 3½" (5.5 cm x 9.5 cm), for blocks and border

From the assorted dark beige prints, cut a *total* of:
- 68 rectangles, each 2" x 3½" (5.5 cm x 9.5 cm), for blocks and border

From the assorted light beige prints, cut a *total* of:
- 144 rectangles, each 2" x 3½" (5.5 cm x 9.5 cm), for blocks and border

From the rust print, cut:
- 7 strips, each 2½" (6.5 cm) wide, for binding

MAKING THE BLOCKS

YOU'LL NEED a total of 48 pieced blocks for this quilt. Avoid duplicating prints within the units and blocks.

1. Sew the dark autumn-toned print rectangles, dark beige print rectangles, and light beige print rectangles to make the units shown. Press the seams as indicated by the arrows. Make 148 of unit A, 68 of unit B, and 72 of unit C.

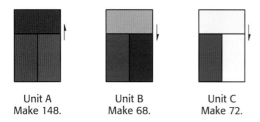

Unit A
Make 148.

Unit B
Make 68.

Unit C
Make 72.

2. For block 1, arrange units A, B, and C in 2 rows as shown. Sew the units into rows. Press the seams as indicated by the arrows. Sew the rows together to complete the block; press. Make 24 of block 1.

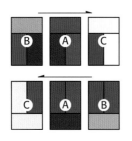

Block 1
Make 24.

3. For block 2, arrange units A, B, and C in 2 rows as shown. Sew and press as for block 1. Make 10 of block 2.

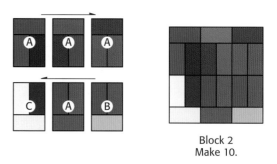

Block 2
Make 10.

4. For block 3, arrange units A, B, and C in 2 rows as shown. Sew and press as for block 1. Make 10 of block 3.

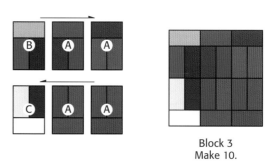

Block 3
Make 10.

5. For block 4, arrange units A and C in 2 rows as shown. Sew and press as for block 1. Make 4 of block 4.

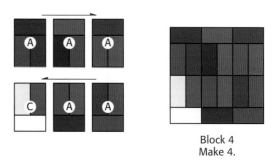

Block 4
Make 4.

ASSEMBLING THE QUILT

1. Refer to the quilt assembly diagram below. Arrange the blocks in 8 horizontal rows of 6 blocks each, making sure to rotate alternate (block 1) blocks within each row as shown. The illusion of a border is created by alternating block 2 and block 3 units and by rotating block 4 units in the quilt corners.

2. Sew the blocks together into rows. Press the seams in opposite directions from row to row.

3. Pin and sew the rows together; press.

FINISHING

1. Divide the backing fabric crosswise into 2 equal panels of approximately 58" (155 cm) each. Join the panels to make a single large backing panel.

2. Center and layer the quilt top and batting over the backing; baste.

3. Quilt as desired.

4. Use the 2½" (6.5 cm) -wide binding strips to make the binding. Sew the binding to the quilt.

Assembly Diagram

DOWN MEMORY LANE

BY MARGARET ROLFE

MARGARET ENJOYS THE *charm of 1930s print fabrics and quilts, a taste triggered by sleeping under a beautiful 1930s quilt while staying in Athens, Georgia. The grandmother of her hostess had made the quilt, and it was a treasured family heirloom.*

Margaret welcomes the current vogue for '30s reproduction prints and has collected them for many years. The scrap-quilt designs in this book are particularly suited to these prints, although for this quilt, the middle values were used rather than the lightest and darkest of these charming prints.

FINISHED QUILT SIZE:
63" x 81" (168 cm x 216 cm)

FINISHED BLOCK SIZE:
9" (24 cm) square

BLOCK DESIGN: 18:4

MATERIALS

44" (112 cm) -wide fabric

- 4½ yds. (4.8 m) *total* of assorted medium-value 1930s-style prints for blocks and border
- 1½ yds. (1.6 m) cream solid fabric for blocks and border
- ⅝ yd. (60 cm) green print for binding
- 4¾ yds. (4.6 cm) print for backing
- 67" x 85" (178 cm x 226 cm) piece of batting

CUTTING

All measurements include ¼" (7.5 mm) -wide seam allowances. Cut binding strips from width of fabric.

From the assorted 1930s-style prints, cut a total of:

- 856 rectangles, each 2" x 3½" (5.5 cm x 9.5 cm), for blocks and border

From the cream solid, cut:

- 278 rectangles, each 2" x 3½" (5.5 cm x 9.5 cm), for blocks and border

From the green print, cut:

- 8 strips, each 2½" (6.5 cm) wide, for binding

MAKING THE BLOCKS

YOU'LL NEED a total of 48 pieced blocks for this quilt. Avoid duplicating prints within the units and blocks.

1. Sew the 1930s-style print rectangles and cream solid rectangles to make the units shown. Press the seams as indicated by the arrows. Make 100 of unit A, 182 of unit B, and 96 of unit C.

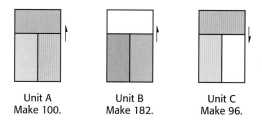

Unit A
Make 100.

Unit B
Make 182.

Unit C
Make 96.

2. Arrange units A, B, and C in 2 rows as shown on page 68. Sew the units into rows. Press the seams as indicated by the arrows.

3. Sew the rows together to complete the block; press. Make 48 blocks.

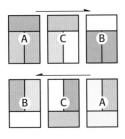
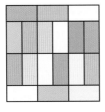
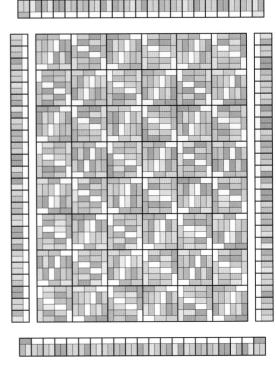

Make 48.

ASSEMBLING THE QUILT

1. Refer to the quilt assembly diagram at right. Arrange the blocks in 8 horizontal rows of 6 blocks each, making sure to rotate blocks within each row as shown.

2. Sew the blocks together into rows. Press the seams in opposite directions from row to row.

3. Pin and sew the rows together; press.

4. Arrange 24 of unit B in a row to make a side border unit as shown. Sew the units together and press the seams to one side. Make 2 border units.

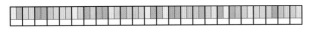

Make 2 side borders.

5. Arrange 2 of unit A and 19 of unit B in a row to make a top/bottom border unit as shown. Sew the units together, and press the seams to one side. Make 2 border units.

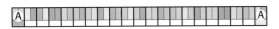

Make a top and a bottom border.

6. Sew border units from step 4 to the sides of the quilt top. Press the seams toward the border units. Repeat to sew border units from step 5 to the top and bottom of the quilt top; press.

Assembly Diagram

FINISHING

1. Divide the backing fabric crosswise into 2 equal panels of approximately 85" (230 cm) each. Join the panels to make a single large backing panel.

2. Center and layer the quilt top and batting over the backing; baste.

3. Quilt as desired.

4. Use the 2½" (6.5 cm) -wide binding strips to make the binding. Sew the binding to the quilt.

SPECTRUM

BY JUDY TURNER

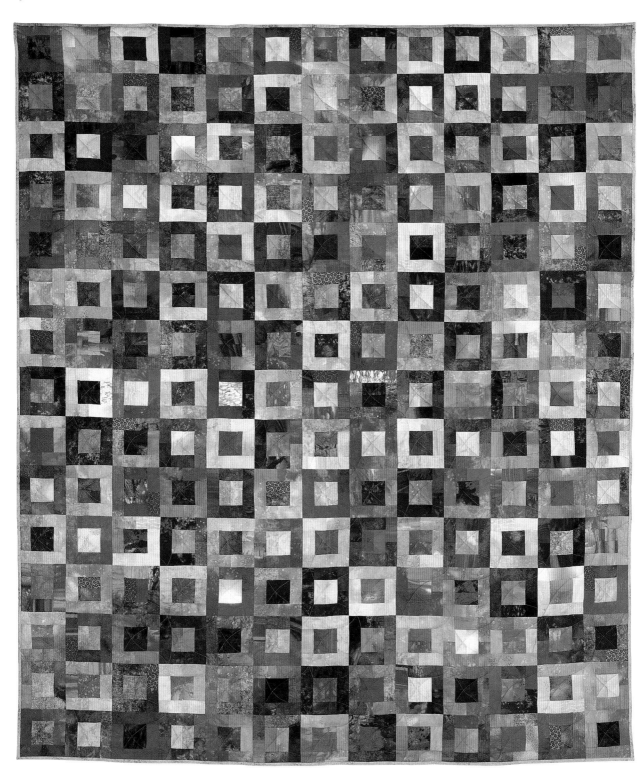

*J*UDY LOVED MAKING *this quilt, as it gave her the opportunity to do her favorite thing: play with color. The quilt is made from a rainbow of lovely hand-dyed and subtly colored prints. To further increase the range of fabrics, she has used the reverse side of most of the fabrics as well.*

This quilt is unlike many of the other quilts in this book in that it is not made from two distinct groups of dark and light fabrics. Rather, Judy incorporates a wide range of fabrics, still carefully maintaining a contrast in value between the two used within each block. Many fabrics are used as both a dark and a light, depending on the value of their neighbors. In some places, the color bleeds from one part of the block to another, or it bleeds between two adjacent blocks. This color bleeding adds interest to the quilt by blurring the pattern a little.

FINISHED QUILT SIZE:
78" x 90" (208 cm x 240 cm)

FINISHED BLOCK SIZE:
6" (16 cm) square

BLOCK DESIGN: 8:1

MATERIALS

44" (112 cm) -wide fabric
- 8½ yds. (8.7 m) *total* of assorted hand-dyed and/or subtle prints in a range of colors and values for blocks
- ¾ yd. (70 cm) gold solid fabric for binding
- 5¼ yds. (5.1 m) print for backing
- 82" x 94" (218 cm x 250 cm) piece of batting

CUTTING

All measurements include ¼" (7.5 mm) -wide seam allowances. Cut binding strips from width of fabric.

From the assorted hand-dyed and/or subtle prints, cut a *total* of:
- 1560 rectangles, each 2" x 3½" (5.5 cm x 9.5 cm), for blocks

From the gold solid, cut:
- 9 strips, each 2½" (6.5 cm) wide, for binding

If you have any special hand-dyed fabrics that you'd rather not cut into rectangles, you may substitute 3½" x 3½" (9.5 cm x 9.5 cm) squares for some of the block centers instead.

Making the Blocks

You'll need a total of 195 pieced blocks for this quilt. Avoid duplicating fabrics within the blocks.

1. For block 1, arrange 2 darker and 6 lighter hand-dyed and/or subtle print rectangles as shown. Blend the colors through the lighter and darker areas of each block (see "Blending" on page 14), occasionally changing the color as it blends around the outer row. Sew the rectangles together; press. Make 98 of block 1.

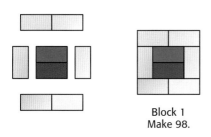

Block 1
Make 98.

2. For block 2, arrange 6 darker and 2 lighter hand-dyed and/or subtle print rectangles as shown. Blend the colors through the lighter and darker areas of each block (see "Blending" on page 14), occasionally changing the color as it blends around the outer row. Sew the rectangles together; press. Make 97 of block 2.

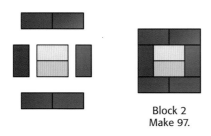

Block 2
Make 97.

Assembling the Quilt

1. Refer to the quilt assembly diagram below. Arrange the blocks in 15 horizontal rows of 13 blocks each, making sure to alternate and rotate the blocks as shown.

2. Sew the blocks together into rows. Press the seams in opposite directions from row to row.

3. Pin and sew the rows together; press.

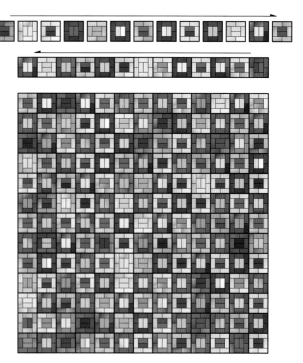

Assembly Diagram

Finishing

1. Divide the backing fabric crosswise into 2 equal panels of approximately 94" (255 cm) each. Join the panels to make a single large backing panel.

2. Center and layer the quilt top and batting over the backing; baste.

3. Quilt as desired.

4. Use the 2½" (6.5 cm) -wide binding strips to make the binding. Sew the binding to the quilt.

INDIGO WEAVE

BY JUDY TURNER

J UDY COMBINED HER *collection of indigo fabrics with a mix of plaids and stripes—an unusual choice that illustrates that "safe is not always best" when it comes to scrap quilts! A large range of tonal values is used in the light areas of the quilt, to the point where the pattern is almost—but not quite—lost. The resultant blurring of the pattern creates visual interest, which is enhanced by a sprinkling of rust-colored prints among the dark indigos.*

FINISHED QUILT SIZE:
44" x 62" (117 cm x 165 cm)

FINISHED BLOCK SIZE:
9" (24 cm) square

BLOCK DESIGN: 18:2

MATERIALS

44" (112 cm) -wide fabric
- 1¼ yds. (1.4 cm) *total* of assorted dark indigo prints for blocks
- A few scraps of rust prints for blocks
- 1 yd. (1.1 m) *total* of assorted light checked and striped prints for blocks
- ¼ yd. (30 cm) rust solid for inner border
- ⅝ yd. (60 cm) blue Japanese print for outer border
- ½ yd. (50 cm) navy solid for binding
- 2¾ yds. (2.6 m) print for backing
- 48" x 66" (127 cm x 175 cm) piece of batting

CUTTING

All measurements include ¼" (7.5 mm) -wide seam allowances. Cut border and binding strips across width of fabric.

From the assorted indigo prints and rust print scraps, cut a *total* of:
- 240 rectangles, each 2" x 3½" (5.5 cm x 9.5 cm), for blocks

From the assorted light checked and striped prints, cut a *total* of:
- 192 rectangles, each 2" x 3½" (5.5 cm x 9.5 cm), for blocks

From the rust solid, cut:
- 5 strips, each 1½" (4 cm) wide, for inner border

From the blue Japanese print, cut:
- 5 strips, each 3½" (9.5 cm) wide, for outer border

From the navy solid, cut:
- 6 strips, each 2½" (6.5 cm) wide, for binding

MAKING THE BLOCKS

YOU'LL NEED a total of 24 pieced blocks for this quilt. Avoid duplicating prints within the block.

1. Arrange 10 indigo print and 8 light checked and striped print rectangles as shown. Occasionally substitute a rust print rectangle for an indigo print rectangle.

2. Sew the rectangles together; press. Make 24 blocks.

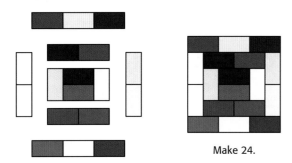

Make 24.

ASSEMBLING THE QUILT

1. Refer to the quilt assembly diagram at right. Arrange the blocks in 6 horizontal rows of 4 blocks each, making sure to scatter the blocks with rust print rectangles over the quilt. Rotate alternate blocks within each row as shown.

2. Sew the blocks together into rows. Press the seams in opposite directions from row to row.

3. Pin and sew the rows together; press.

4. Refer to "Border Strips with Butted Corners" (page 44) to fit and sew the 1½" (4 cm) -wide rust inner borders to the quilt. Press the seams toward the borders.

5. Repeat step 4 and sew the 3½" (9.5 cm) -wide blue Japanese print outer border strips to the quilt. Press the seams toward the outer borders.

Assembly Diagram

FINISHING

1. Divide the backing fabric crosswise into 2 equal panels of approximately 49" (130 cm) each. Join the panels to make a single large backing panel.

2. Center and layer the quilt top and batting over the backing; baste.

3. Quilt as desired.

4. Use the 2½" (6.5 cm) -wide binding strips to make the binding. Sew the binding to the quilt.

BONDI BEACH

BY MARGARET ROLFE. QUILTED BY JACKIE MacNAB.

THE VIBRANT BLUES *and yellows in this quilt evoke the colors of Australian beaches, where the blue sky and sea contrast with the golden yellow of the sand and sunshine. The simple pattern creates starlike crosses at the corners of the blocks, and the quilt finishes with a pieced border of blue, reminiscent of the water lapping the edge of the sand.*

FINISHED QUILT SIZE:
96" x 96" (240 cm x 240 cm)

FINISHED BLOCK SIZE:
8" (20 cm) square

BLOCK DESIGN: 8:2

MATERIALS

44" (112 cm) -wide fabric

- 6¾ yds. (5.6 m) *total* of assorted yellow prints, including some with blue, for blocks
- 4¾ yds. (3.9 m) *total* of assorted blue prints, including some with yellow, for blocks
- ¾ yd. (70 cm) blue print for binding
- 8½ yds. (7.6 m) print for backing
- 100" x 100" (250 cm x 250 cm) piece of batting

CUTTING

All measurements include ¼" (7.5 mm) -wide seam allowances. Cut binding strips across width of fabric.

From the assorted yellow prints, cut a *total* of:
- 724 rectangles, each 2½" x 4½" (6.5 cm x 11.5 cm), for blocks

From the assorted blue prints, cut a *total* of:
- 428 rectangles, each 2½" x 4½" (6.5 cm x 11.5 cm), for blocks

From the blue print for binding, cut:
- 10 strips, each 2½" (6.5 cm) wide

MAKING THE BLOCKS

YOU'LL NEED a total of 144 pieced blocks for this quilt. Avoid duplicating fabrics within the blocks.

1. For block 1, arrange 6 yellow print and 2 blue print rectangles as shown. Sew the rectangles together; press. Make 64 of block 1.

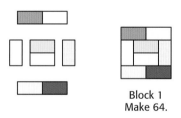

Block 1
Make 64.

2. For block 2, arrange 7 yellow print rectangles and 1 blue print rectangle as shown. Sew the rectangles together; press. Make 36 of block 2.

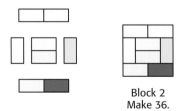

Block 2
Make 36.

3. For block 3, arrange 2 yellow print and 6 blue print rectangles in 2 rows as shown. Sew the rectangles into rows. Press the seams as indicated by the arrows. Sew the rows together to complete the block; press. Make 40 of block 3.

Block 3
Make 40.

4. For block 4, arrange 2 yellow print and 6 blue print rectangles in 2 rows as shown. Sew the rectangles into rows. Press the seams as indicated by the arrows. Sew the rows together to complete the block; press. Make 4 of Block 4.

Block 4
Make 4.

ASSEMBLING THE QUILT

1. Refer to the quilt assembly diagram above right. Arrange the blocks in 12 horizontal rows of 12 blocks each, making sure to rotate the block 1 and block 2 units as shown. A border is created by placing block 3 units around the perimeter of the quilt top and finishing the corners with rotated block 4 units.

2. Sew the blocks together into rows. Press the seams in opposite directions from row to row.

3. Pin and sew the rows together; press.

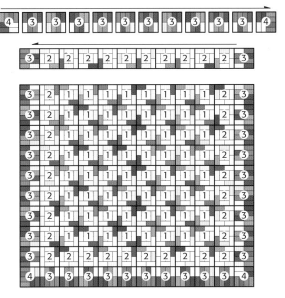

Assembly Diagram

FINISHING

1. Divide the backing fabric crosswise into 3 equal panels of approximately 102" (250 cm) each. Join the panels to make a single large backing panel.

2. Center and layer the quilt top and batting over the backing; baste.

3. Quilt as desired.

4. Use the 2½" (6.5 cm) -wide binding strips to make the binding. Sew the binding to the quilt.

CHECKERBOARD

BY JUDY TURNER

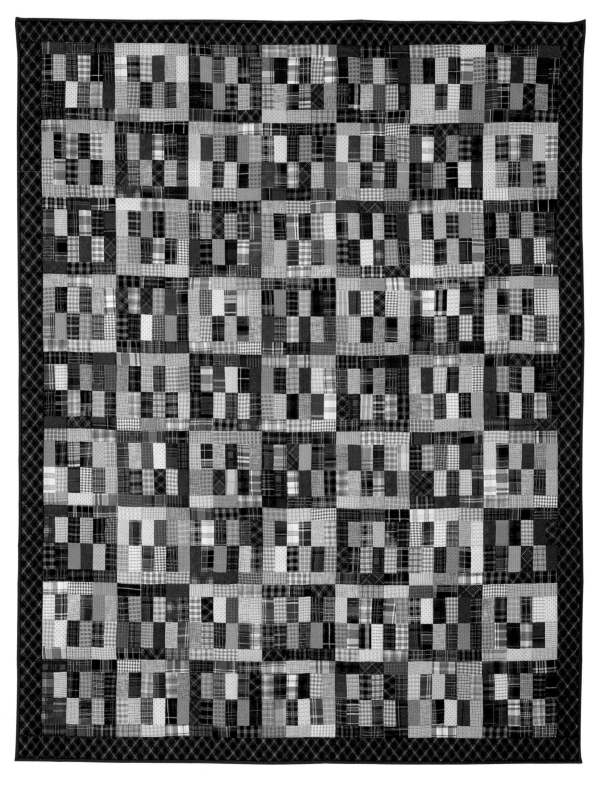

JUDY USED A *combination of dark and light geometric prints to make this all-check-and-plaid quilt. Deep blue, burgundy, purple, and black fabrics add richness and depth, while a whole range of light colors give the quilt a warm glow. To maintain the intensity of color, you'll want to do as Judy has done and avoid fabrics with lots of white in them.*

FINISHED QUILT SIZE:
68½" x 86½" (182 cm x 230 cm)

FINISHED BLOCK SIZE:
9" (24 cm) square

BLOCK DESIGN: 18:6

MATERIALS

44" (112 cm) -wide fabric
- 3 yds. (3.2 m) *total* of assorted dark checked and plaid prints for blocks
- 3 yds. (3.2 m) *total* of assorted light checked and plaid prints for blocks
- ⅞ yd. (80 cm) burgundy plaid for border
- ⅝ yd. (60 cm) blue solid for binding
- 5¼ yds. (4.8 m) print for backing
- 73" x 91" (192 cm x 240 cm) piece of batting

CUTTING

All measurements include ¼" (7.5 mm) -wide seam allowances. Cut borders and binding strips across width of fabric.

From the assorted dark checked and plaid prints, cut a *total* of:
- 572 rectangles, each 2" x 3½" (5.5 cm x 9.5 cm), for blocks

From the assorted light checked and plaid prints, cut a *total* of:
- 562 rectangles, each 2" x 3½" (5.5 cm x 9.5 cm), for blocks

From the burgundy plaid, cut:
- 8 strips, each 3¼" (8.5 cm) wide, for border

From the blue solid, cut:
- 8 strips, each 2½" (6.5 cm) wide, for binding

MAKING THE BLOCKS

YOU'LL NEED a total of 63 pieced blocks for this quilt. Avoid duplicating prints within the units and blocks.

1. Sew the dark and light checked and plaid print rectangles to make the units shown, making sure there is a strong light/dark contrast in each unit and block (where applicable); press the seams as indicated by the arrows. Make 128 of unit A, 64 of unit B, 124 of unit C, and 62 of unit D.

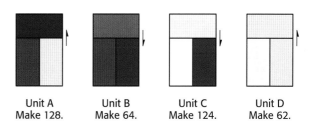

Unit A
Make 128.

Unit B
Make 64.

Unit C
Make 124.

Unit D
Make 62.

2. For block 1, arrange units A and B in 2 rows as shown. Sew the units into rows. Press the seams as indicated by the arrows. Sew the rows together to complete the block; press. Make 32 of block 1.

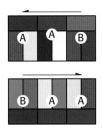
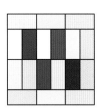

Block 1
Make 32.

3. For block 2, arrange units C and D in 2 rows as shown. Sew and press as for block 1. Make 31 of block 2.

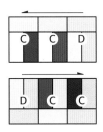

Block 2
Make 31.

> Once the units are laid out into their position in a block, it may be necessary to re-press some of the seam allowances within the units so that they interlock.

ASSEMBLING THE QUILT

1. Refer to the quilt assembly diagram at right. Arrange the blocks in 9 horizontal rows of 7 blocks each, making sure to alternate the blocks within each row as shown. Avoid placing the same prints next to each other, and scatter the colors over the quilt.

2. Sew the blocks together into rows. Press the seams in opposite directions from row to row.

3. Pin and sew the rows together; press.

4. Refer to "Border Strips with Butted Corners" (page 44) to fit and sew the 3¼" (8.5 cm) -wide burgundy plaid borders to the quilt. Press the seams toward the borders.

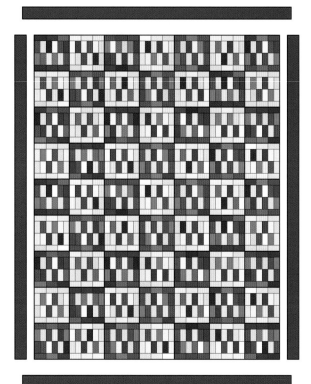

Assembly Diagram

FINISHING

1. Divide the backing fabric crosswise into 2 equal panels of approximately 95" (240 cm) each. Join the panels to make a single large backing panel.

2. Center and layer the quilt top and batting over the backing; baste.

3. Quilt as desired.

4. Use the 2½" (6.5 cm) -wide binding strips to make the binding. Sew the binding to the quilt.

1-2-3 WHAT CAN YOU SEE?

BY JUDY TURNER

This is a *cheerful—and educational!—*quilt for a toddler's first bed. The child can take great delight in making discoveries among the various picture prints while at the same time developing language skills. The bright backgrounds of the many prints are grouped together by color, bringing order and unity to the overall design.

FINISHED QUILT SIZE:
63" x 77" (158 cm x 193 cm)

FINISHED BLOCK SIZE:
4" x 6" (10 cm x 15 cm)

BLOCK DESIGN: 3:2

MATERIALS

44" (112 cm) -wide fabric
- 1¼ yds. (1 m) *total* of assorted bright blue prints, including juvenile motifs, for blocks
- 1¼ yds. (1 m) *total* of assorted prints with white backgrounds, including juvenile prints, for blocks
- 1¼ yds. (1 m) *total* of assorted bright pink prints, including juvenile motifs, for blocks
- 1¼ yds. (1 m) *total* of assorted bright yellow prints, including juvenile motifs, for blocks
- ¼ yd. (30 cm) yellow solid fabric for inner border
- 1¼ yds. (1.2 m) blue print for outer border
- ⅝ yd. (60 cm) blue solid for binding
- 3¾ yds. (3.4 m) print for backing
- 67" x 81" (168 cm x 203 cm) piece of batting

CUTTING

All measurements include ¼" (7.5 mm) -wide seam allowances. Cut border and binding strips across width of fabric.

From the assorted bright blue prints, cut a *total* of:
- 108 rectangles, each 2½" x 4½" (6.5 cm x 11.5 cm), for blocks*

From the assorted prints with white backgrounds, cut a *total* of:
- 108 rectangles, each 2½" x 4½" (6.5 cm x 11.5 cm), for blocks*

From the assorted bright pink prints, cut a *total* of:
- 108 rectangles, each 2½" x 4½" (6.5 cm x 11.5 cm), for blocks*

From the assorted bright yellow prints, cut a *total* of:
- 105 rectangles, each 2½" x 4½" (6.5 cm x 11.5 cm), for blocks*

From the yellow solid, cut:
- 8 strips, each 1" (3 cm) wide, for inner border

From the blue print, cut:
- 8 strips, each 5½" (14 cm) wide, for outer border

From the blue solid, cut:
- 8 strips, each 2½" (6.5 cm) wide, for binding

*Cut juvenile prints so motifs fit within rectangle size, regardless of grain. There will be some fabric waste, and extra fabric has been allowed in the yardage for this.

MAKING THE BLOCKS

YOU'LL NEED a total of 143 pieced blocks for this quilt. Avoid duplicating prints within the blocks.

Sew the blue, white, pink, and yellow print rectangles in groups of 3 to make the blocks shown, combining the on-grain rectangles with those cut off-grain to stabilize the seams. Press the seams as indicated by the arrows. Make 36 each of blocks 1, 2, and 3, and 35 of block 4.

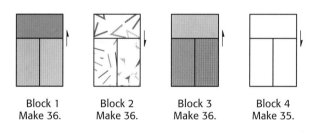

Block 1
Make 36.

Block 2
Make 36.

Block 3
Make 36.

Block 4
Make 35.

Handle off-grain rectangles and the resulting units with care so as not to stretch the bias edges.

ASSEMBLING THE QUILT

1. Refer to the quilt assembly diagram at right. Arrange the blocks in 11 horizontal rows of 13 blocks each, making sure to alternate the blocks by color within the rows as shown.

2. Sew the blocks together into rows. Press the seams in opposite directions from row to row.

3. Pin and sew the rows together; press.

4. Refer to "Border Strips with Mitered Corners" (page 45) to measure, trim, fit, and sew inner/outer border units to the quilt. Use the 1" (3 cm) -wide yellow strips for the inner border and the 5½" (14 cm) -wide blue print strips for the outer border. Press the seams toward the border units.

Assembly Diagram

FINISHING

1. Divide the backing fabric crosswise into 2 equal panels of approximately 67" (170 cm) each. Join the panels to make a single large backing panel.

2. Center and layer the quilt top and batting over the backing; baste.

3. Quilt as desired.

4. Use the 2½" (6.5 cm) -wide binding strips to make the binding. Sew the binding to the quilt.

BENTO BOX

BY JUDY TURNER

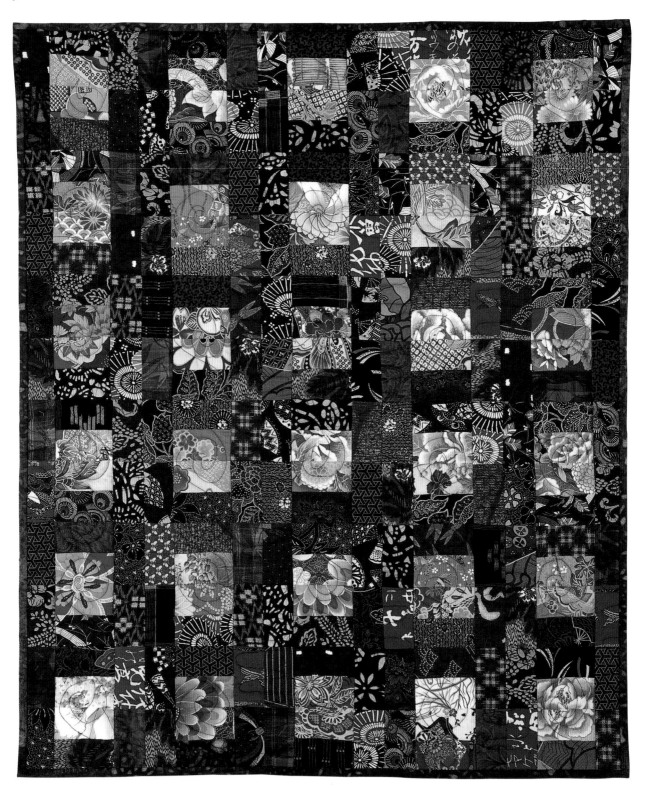

*B*EAUTIFUL JAPANESE PRINTS *are the focus of this quilt, with the dark blue indigos in sharp contrast to the brightly colored floral prints. It is a satisfyingly simple quilt to make and the perfect showcase for a special collection of fabrics. By using the reverse side of many of the indigo fabrics, you'll greatly increase the range of values and prints in the quilt.*

FINISHED QUILT SIZE:
30" x 36" (80 cm x 96 cm)

FINISHED BLOCK SIZE:
6" (16 cm) square

BLOCK DESIGN: 8:6

MATERIALS

44" (112 cm) -wide fabric
- 1 yd. (1 m) *total* of assorted Japanese indigo prints for blocks
- ½ yd. (40 cm) *total* of assorted brightly colored Japanese floral prints for blocks
- ⅜ yd. (30 cm) indigo print for binding
- 1¼ yds. (1.1 m) print for backing
- 34" x 40" (90 cm x 106 cm) piece of batting

CUTTING

All measurements include ¼" (7.5 mm) -wide seam allowances. Cut binding strips across width of fabric.

From the assorted Japanese indigo prints, cut a *total* of:
- 180 rectangles, each 2" x 3½" (5.5 cm x 9.5 cm), for blocks

From the assorted brightly colored Japanese floral prints, cut a *total* of:
- 60 rectangles, each 2" x 3½" (5.5 cm x 9.5 cm), for blocks

From the indigo print, cut:
- 4 strips, each 2½" (6.5 cm) wide, for binding

MAKING THE BLOCKS

YOU'LL NEED a total of 30 pieced blocks for this quilt. Avoid duplicating prints within the blocks.

1. Arrange 6 indigo print and 2 floral print rectangles as shown. Blend the colors and patterns of the floral prints in the center of each block (see "Blending" on page 14).

2. Sew the rectangles together; press. Make 30 blocks.

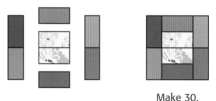

Make 30.

ASSEMBLING THE QUILT

1. Refer to the quilt assembly diagram below. Arrange the blocks in 6 horizontal rows of 5 blocks each as shown.

2. Sew the blocks together into rows. Press the seams in opposite directions from row to row.

3. Pin and sew the rows together; press.

FINISHING

1. Center and layer the quilt top and batting over the backing; baste.

2. Quilt as desired.

3. Use the 2½" (6.5 cm) -wide binding strips to make the binding. Sew the binding to the quilt.

Assembly Diagram

LAVA FLOW

BY MARGARET ROLFE. QUILTED BY BETH REID.

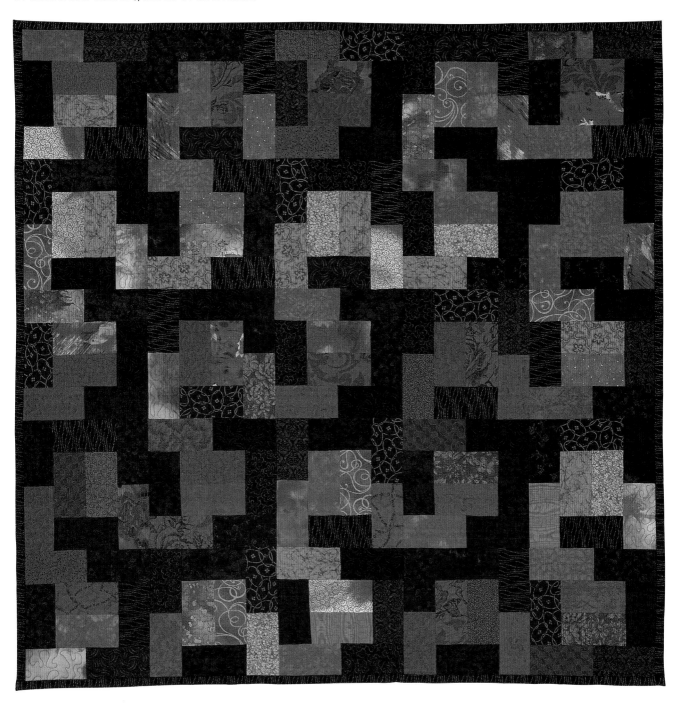

THE BLOCK IN *this quilt creates wonderful sinuous curves when the blocks are rotated and alternated. The strong, hot colors of the pink and orange fabrics reminded Margaret of molten lava flowing from an active volcano, but any group of related colors would be equally effective in this design.*

FINISHED QUILT SIZE:
40" x 40" (100 cm x 100 cm)

FINISHED BLOCK SIZE:
8" (20 cm) square

BLOCK DESIGN: 8:5

MATERIALS

44" (112 cm) -wide fabric
- 1 yd. (80 cm) *total* of assorted black and navy prints for blocks
- 1 yd. (80 cm) *total* of assorted bright pink, orange, red, and purple prints for blocks
- ½ yd. (40 cm) navy print for binding
- 1¼ yds. (1.1 m) print for backing
- 44" x 44" (110 cm x 110 cm) piece of batting

CUTTING

All measurements include ¼" (7.5 mm) -wide seam allowances. Cut binding strips across width of fabric.

From the assorted black and navy prints, cut a *total* of:
- 100 rectangles, each 2½" x 4½" (6.5 cm x 11.5 cm), for blocks

From the assorted bright pink, orange, red, and purple prints, cut a *total* of:
- 100 rectangles, each 2½" x 4½" (6.5 cm x 11.5 cm), for blocks

From the navy print, cut:
- 5 strips, each 3" (8 cm) wide, for binding

MAKING THE BLOCKS

YOU'LL NEED a total of 25 pieced blocks for this quilt. Avoid duplicating prints within the blocks.

1. Arrange 4 black and navy print and 4 pink, orange, red, and purple print rectangles as shown. Shade the pink, orange, red, and purple prints from light to dark, juxtaposing the pinks with oranges, and the reds with purples to increase the vibrancy of the color.

2. Sew the rectangles together; press. Make 25 blocks.

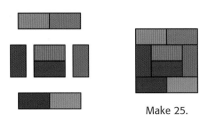

Make 25.

ASSEMBLING THE QUILT

1. Refer to the quilt assembly diagram below. Arrange the blocks in 5 horizontal rows of 5 blocks each as shown. Make sure to rotate the blocks within each row as shown. Place the blocks so that the different values of the red prints flow through the "curves."

2. Sew the blocks together into rows. Press the seams in opposite directions from row to row.

3. Pin and sew the rows together; press.

FINISHING

1. Center and layer the quilt top and batting over the backing; baste.

2. Quilt as desired.

3. Use the 3" (8 cm) -wide binding strips to make the binding. Sew the binding to the quilt.

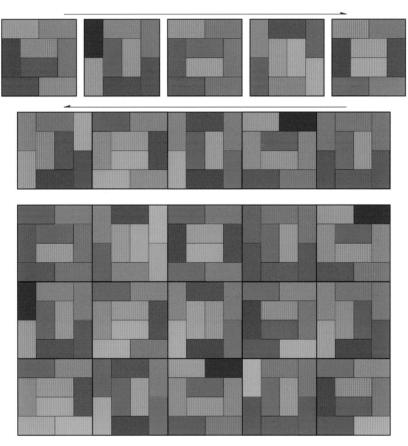

Assembly Diagram

SIMPLY SCRAPS

BY JUDY TURNER

I INEVITABLY, THERE ARE *some leftovers when scrap quilts are made. This super-simple quilt was made using the leftovers of both Judy's and Margaret's other quilts, so it contains a wide assortment of fabrics. Judy sorted the rectangles into lights and darks, then grouped them into pairs by color. She focused on the red, blue, green, yellow, white, and black rectangles and rejected others, such as some of the browns and pinks. The red and yellow fabrics are important accents and are therefore scattered throughout the quilt.*

FINISHED QUILT SIZE:
59½" x 76" (158 cm x 202 cm)

FINISHED BLOCK SIZE:
3" x 4½" (8 cm x 12 cm)

BLOCK DESIGN: 3:1

MATERIALS

44" (112 cm) -wide fabric

- 2¼ yds. (2.2 m) *total* of assorted dark prints for blocks
- 2 yds. (2.1 m) *total* of assorted light prints for blocks
- ¼ yd. (30 cm) yellow solid for inner border
- 2 yds. (1.9 m) red print for outer border and binding
- 3¾ yds. (3.4 m) print for backing
- 64" x 80" (168 cm x 212 cm) piece of batting

CUTTING

All measurements include ¼" (7.5 mm) -wide seam allowances. Cut inner border strips across width of fabric; cut outer border and binding strips along length of fabric (parallel to selvage).

From the assorted dark prints, cut a *total* of:
- 390 rectangles, each 2" x 3½" (5.5 cm x 9.5 cm), for blocks

From the assorted light prints, cut a *total* of:
- 375 rectangles, each 2" x 3½" (5.5 cm x 9.5 cm), for blocks

From the yellow solid, cut:
- 6 strips (8 for metric), each 1¼" (3.5 cm) wide, for inner border

From the red print, cut:
- 4 strips, each 4" (10.5 cm) wide, for outer border
- 4 strips, each 2½" (6.5 cm) wide, for binding

Making the Blocks

You'll need a total of 255 pieced blocks for this quilt. Avoid duplicating prints within the blocks.

Sew the dark and light print rectangles to make the blocks shown, making sure there is a strong light/dark contrast in each block. Pair rectangles of the same color to make the square section of each block, and finish the block with a rectangle of contrasting value. Press the seams as indicated by the arrows. Make 135 of block 1 and 120 of block 2.

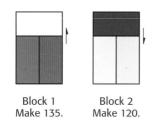

Block 1
Make 135.

Block 2
Make 120.

Assembling the Quilt

1. Refer to the quilt assembly diagram at right. Arrange the blocks in 15 horizontal rows of 17 blocks each, making sure to alternate the blocks as shown and to scatter the various colors over the quilt.

2. Sew the blocks together into rows. Press the seams in opposite directions from row to row.

3. Pin and sew the rows together; press.

4. Refer to "Border Strips with Butted Corners" (page 44) to fit and sew the 1¼" (3.5 cm) -wide yellow solid inner borders to the quilt. Press the seams toward the borders.

5. Repeat step 4 to fit and sew the 4" (10.5 cm) -wide red print outer border strips to the quilt. Press the seams toward the outer borders.

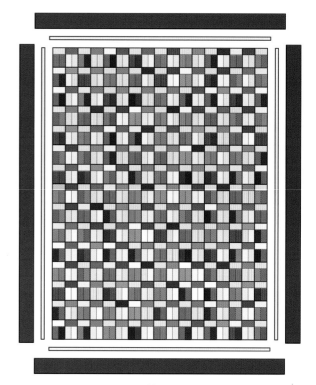

Assembly Diagram

Finishing

1. Divide the backing fabric crosswise into 2 equal panels of approximately 67" (170 cm) each. Join the panels to make a single large backing panel.

2. Center and layer the quilt top and batting over the backing; baste.

3. Quilt as desired.

4. Use the 2½" (6.5 cm) -wide binding strips to make the binding. Sew the binding to the quilt.

CHRISTMAS LANTERNS

BY MARGARET ROLFE. QUILTED BY BETH REID.

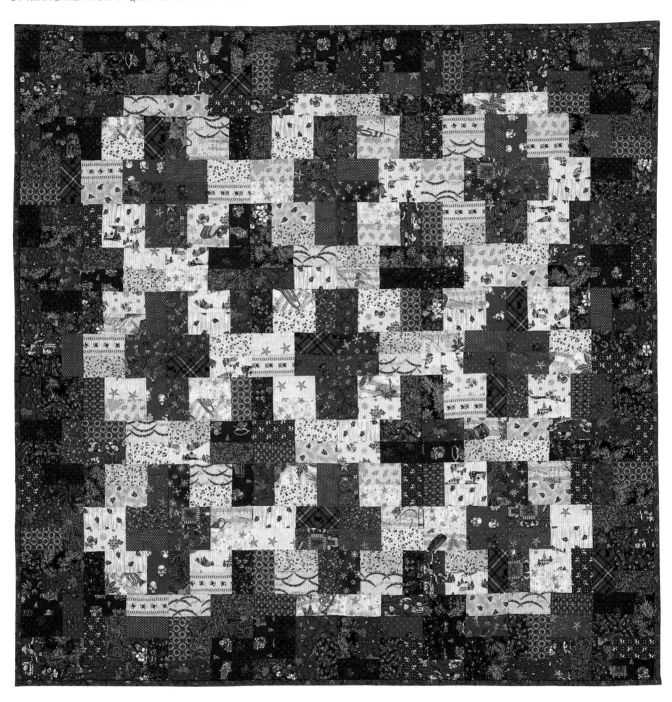

I T IS LOVELY *to have special quilts that only come out to celebrate holidays, such as Christmas. Margaret liked the way that simply reversing these blocks made lanternlike shapes. A further touch of red is introduced by adding a border pattern that resembles a threaded ribbon. Although Margaret used her collection of Christmas prints for this quilt, she also added other complementary red, green, and beige prints.*

FINISHED QUILT SIZE:
45" x 45" (120 cm x 120 cm)

FINISHED BLOCK SIZE:
6" (16 cm) square

BLOCK DESIGN: 8:4

MATERIALS

44" (112 cm) -wide fabric
- ½ yd. (40 cm) red print for blocks and binding
- ⅝ yd. (60 cm) *total* of assorted red Christmas and related prints for blocks and border
- 1¼ yds. (1.2 m) *total* of assorted green Christmas and related prints for blocks and border
- ¾ yd. (80 cm) *total* of assorted beige Christmas and related prints for blocks
- 2¾ yds. (2.6 m) print for backing
- 49" x 49" (130 cm x 130 cm) piece of batting

CUTTING

All measurements include ¼" (7.5 mm) -wide seam allowances. Cut binding strips across width of fabric.

From the red print, cut:
- 5 strips, each 2½" (6.5 cm) wide, for binding

From the red prints, including remaining red print from binding, cut a *total* of:
- 97 rectangles, each 2" x 3½" (5.5 cm x 9.5 cm), for blocks and borders

From the green prints, cut a *total* of:
- 209 rectangles, each 2" x 3½" (5.5 cm x 9.5 cm), for blocks and borders

From the beige prints, cut a *total* of:
- 144 rectangles, each 2" x 3½" (5.5 cm x 9.5 cm), for blocks

MAKING THE BLOCKS

YOU'LL NEED a total of 36 pieced blocks for this quilt. Avoid duplicating prints within the blocks and units.

1. For block 1, arrange 2 green, 4 beige, and 2 red print rectangles as shown. Sew the rectangles together; press. Make 18 of block 1.

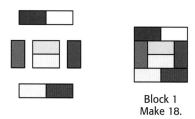

Block 1
Make 18.

2. For block 2, arrange 2 green, 4 beige, and 2 red print rectangles as shown. Sew and press as for block 1. Make 18 of block 2.

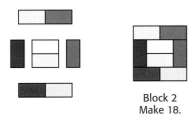

Block 2
Make 18.

ASSEMBLING THE QUILT

1. Refer to the quilt assembly diagram at right. Arrange the blocks in 6 horizontal rows of 6 blocks each, alternating and rotating the blocks as shown.

2. Sew the blocks together into rows. Press the seams in opposite directions from row to row.

3. Pin and sew the rows together; press.

4. Sew the remaining green and red print rectangles to make the units shown. Press the seams as indicated by the arrows. Make 29 of unit A and 25 of unit B.

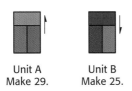

Unit A
Make 29.

Unit B
Make 25.

5. Arrange 8 of unit A and 7 of unit B in a row to make the left border as shown. Sew the units together and press the seams to one side. Label the border. Repeat to arrange, sew, and press 9 of unit A and 6 of B to make the right border as shown. Label the border.

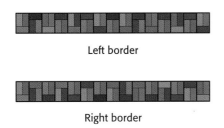

Left border

Right border

6. Arrange 6 each of units A and B in a row to make the top border as shown. Sew the units together and press the seams to one side. Label the border. Repeat to arrange, sew, and press 6 each of units A and B to make the bottom border as shown. Label the border.

Top border

Bottom border

7. Sew the border from step 6 to the top and bottom of the quilt; press the seams toward the border. Repeat to sew the border from step 5 to the appropriate sides of the quilt top; press toward the border.

Assembly Diagram

FINISHING

1. Divide the backing fabric crosswise into 2 equal panels of approximately 49" (130 cm) each. Join the panels to make a single large backing panel.

2. Center and layer the quilt top and batting over the backing; baste.

3. Quilt as desired.

4. Use the 2½" (6.5 cm) -wide binding strips to make the binding. Sew the binding to the quilt.

ABOUT THE AUTHORS

Judy Turner

Margaret Rolfe

Judy Turner and Margaret Rolfe met when Judy took a class from Margaret in the early 1980s, and they have been friends ever since. Both are committed to quiltmaking and both have made it their professional career through exhibiting quilts, teaching, and writing books. Both live in Canberra, Australia's capital city.

Judy is a well-known quilt teacher, giving classes throughout Australia. Her quilts have been exhibited widely in Australia, as well as in Japan, the United States, and Europe. In 1997, she wrote *Awash with Colour* (That Patchwork Place), a book on creating colorwash quilts with fabric strips. Judy has developed a technique of making quilts by couching woolen threads onto a background. She has exhibited many quilts in this style during the past several years, and her woolen quilt "Desert Sky" was selected for 1997 Quilt National. Judy loves to play with color and enjoys making quilts that use a multitude of fabrics to create beautiful shaded effects.

Margaret is known worldwide for her books on quiltmaking. Most particularly, she is known for her pieced animal designs, published in many books, including her own *A Quilter's Ark* and *Quilt a Koala* (That Patchwork Place, 1997, and Martingale & Company, 2000). Interested in quilt history, she has researched and written two books on the history of quiltmaking in Australia. In 1999, Margaret teamed with Judy Hooworth to write *Spectacular Scraps* (Martingale & Company). Underlying all Margaret's work is a fascination with pattern, whether patterns made from her beloved animals or patterns used in traditional and scrap quilts. In 2001, Margaret was honored for her contribution to quilting in Australia by being appointed a member of the Order of Australia.